The **Reflective Educator's Guide** to **MENTORING**

For David and Tom, our husbands, closest colleagues, and best friends

The **Reflective Educator's Guide** to **MENTORING**

Strengthening Practice Through Knowledge, Story, and Metaphor

DIANE YENDOL-HOPPEY   NANCY FICHTMAN DANA

Foreword by Jeffrey Glanz

CORWIN PRESS
A SAGE Publications Company
Thousand Oaks, CA 91320

For information:

Corwin Press
A Sage Publications Company
2455 Teller Road
Thousand Oaks, California 91320
www.corwinpress.com

Sage Publications Ltd.
1 Oliver's Yard
55 City Road
London EC1Y 1SP
United Kingdom

Sage Publications India Pvt. Ltd.
B-42, Panchsheel Enclave
Post Box 4109
New Delhi 110 017   India

Printed in the United States of America

Library of Congress Cataloging-in-Publication Data

Yendol-Hoppey, Diane.
The reflective educator's guide to mentoring: Strengthening practice through knowledge, story, and metaphor/Diane Yendol-Hoppey and Nancy Fichtman Dana.
    p. cm.
Includes bibliographical references and index.
ISBN-13: 978-1-4129-3862-4 (cloth: alk. paper)
ISBN-13: 978-1-4129-3863-1 (pbk.: alk. paper)
    1. Mentoring in education. 2. Mentoring in education—Case studies. I. Dana, Nancy Fichtman, 1964- II. Title.
LB1731.4.Y46 2007
371.102—dc22   2006025911

This book is printed on acid-free paper.

06 07 08 09 10   10 9 8 7 6 5 4 3 2 1

Acquisitions Editor:	Faye Zucker
Editorial Assistant:	Gem Rabanera
Production Editor:	Beth A. Bernstein
Copy Editor:	Brenda Weight
Typesetter:	C&M Digitals (P) Ltd.
Proofreader:	Tracy Marcynzsyn
Indexer:	Sylvia Coates
Cover Designer:	Michael Dubowe
Graphic Artist:	Lisa Miller

Contents

Foreword

by Jeffrey Glanz

Dean of Graduate Programs
Wagner College
Staten Island, NY

Michelle Wilk was excited. Having just graduated from a traditional teaching preparation program at a local college, Michelle was fortunate to have secured a position on her first application to a school in the neighborhood in which she lived. One of the better teacher candidates in her program, she earned Student Teacher of the Year honors as an "exemplary educator who knows how to differentiate instruction and treat each child with developmentally appropriate instruction." According to the education chair, "Ms. Wilk is a caring, sensitive, and competent special education teacher."

Impressed with Ms. Wilk, Dr. Esposito, the building principal, assigned her to a CTT (collaborative team teaching) position with Dorothy Davis, the regular education specialist. Although Michelle felt very prepared, she realized after a few short weeks that serving as a real teacher was markedly different from her student teaching experience. She had many questions about school regulations, curricular materials, and instructional policies. She also seemed to have trouble pacing her lessons and multitasking during the rapid pace not uncommon in a CTT classroom.

Ms. Davis wasn't much help because she, too, was relatively new to the school. Dr. Esposito was cordial but, quite honestly, very busy with her duties as principal, especially at the start of the new school year. Michelle was nearly at her wits' end. With no one to go to for assistance, she visited a professor and lamented the fact that she was being "left to sink or swim."

For those of us who entered teaching in the past century (and I mean "long ago" in the past century), learning to teach by the "sink or swim" method is not surprising. Most of us did . . . or didn't. Schools today, however, are significantly more complex for a variety of reasons, as you, the reader, certainly know. Given the crisis of teacher attrition, mentoring—as the authors of this highly readable volume note—is more important than ever. In the words of Diane Yendol-Hoppey and Nancy Fichtman Dana, "Effective mentoring is an essential answer to the daunting attrition rate problem. We need strong mentor teachers, and we need them fast!"

Much of my own research and writing has focused on the critically important responsibility to support teachers, at all levels of development, by engaging them in meaningful, ongoing, structured, and unstructured conversations about teaching practices that promote student learning for all students. Susan Sullivan and I (2006) think that such instructional dialogue is crucial and too often eschewed, for a variety of reasons, by many instructional supervisors and school administrators. Instructional leaders, mentors among them, must remain steadfast and committed to supporting teachers in many ways, and be capable and ready to work with teachers on ways of best promoting student achievement.

These supervisors (be they called assistant principals, principals, staff developers, coaches, peers, or mentors) are specially trained in models of supervision, instructional strategies, curriculum development, observation techniques, support mechanisms for beginning teachers, technological applications that promote teaching and learning, and assessment strategies, among other areas.

A problem I have encountered in working with schools through the years is that such approaches to supervision are taken too lightly and are not performed by individuals with the necessary supervisory skills. Being a successful teacher by itself does not make one, for instance, a good mentor. What is most refreshing about the book you are about to read is that the authors, Yendol-Hoppey and Dana, remain committed to meaningful supervision by specially trained mentors who have the requisite knowledge, skills, and dispositions to serve as strong supports for beginning teachers and who are well versed in many of the supervisory areas noted above.

Mentoring is a process that facilitates instructional improvement wherein an experienced and specially prepared educator works with a novice or less experienced teacher collaboratively and nonjudgmentally to study and deliberate on ways instruction in the classroom may be improved. Mentors are not judges or critics, but facilitators of instructional improvement.

The Reflective Educator's Guide to Mentoring adds significantly to the literature in the field by advocating for such an approach to mentoring. The text is user friendly and interspersed with appropriate anecdotes or stories that catch the reader's attention and make for a very enjoyable and quick read. The volume is well grounded in theory but also is very practical in that the main chapters of the volume offer "glimpses of seven effective mentor teachers." These vignettes are presented in rich detail, providing mentors with concrete suggestions for working with beginning teachers. The greatest value of this volume is, in fact, these case studies or vignettes that inform through real-life examples rather than merely providing a list of dos and don'ts, as some volumes do.

Each chapter is followed by very useful exercises for discussion and exploration that serve to strengthen or deepen reader knowledge of the material. This book is invaluable because it shares the stories of teachers who have really deeply engaged in understanding the nature of their mentoring work with all its intricacies. It honors what we know about teacher supervision. Above all, the book cultivates a mentoring pedagogy that is sound, cutting edge, and, quite simply, makes sense.

I would have written this foreword if just for the reasons I articulated above. But this book has much more to offer because it is aligned to a pedagogic approach, if you will, that frames my own thinking, writing, and practice. The belief in and commitment to constructivism and reflective practice makes this volume all the more worthy. It addresses these ideas not in an overt way but subtly in its approach, format, and philosophy.

Fosnot (1989) writes, "An empowered teacher is a reflective decision maker who finds joy in learning and in investigating the teaching/learning process—one who views learning as construction and teaching as a facilitating process to enhance and enrich development" (p. xi). Fosnet's comments are true for mentors as well. Although not quoting Piaget, Vygotsky, Kohler, Bruner, or Dewey, this volume is true to the values of these great thinkers and their social constructivist orientation. Vygotsky (2002) argued that since knowledge is constructed in a sociocultural context, social interaction, cultural tools, and activity shape individual development and learning. Yendol-Hoppey and Dana know this to be true for the mentor-mentee relationship in teaching. It's reflected in each of the main chapters, as the reader "reads between the lines." It's part and parcel of the very fabric of the approach to mentorship taken by the authors.

Intimately connected to constructivist thought is a most essential pedagogical instrument or process that serves as the catalyst or grounding to actualize constructivism. Reflective practice is at the heart of constructivist theory. Reflection serves to deepen individual experience. Reflective practice permits the individual to construct self-knowledge that may facilitate instructional improvement. Osterman and Kottkamp (2004) summarize best how learning through reflective practice draws from constructivism and experiential learning:

- Learning is an active process requiring involvement of the learner. Knowledge cannot simply be transmitted. For learning to take place, professionals must be motivated to learn and have an active role in determining the direction and progress of learning. Meaningful problems engage people in learning.
- Learning must acknowledge and build on prior experiences and knowledge. Accordingly, professionals need opportunities to explore, articulate, and represent their own ideas and knowledge.
- Learners construct knowledge through experience. Opportunities to observe and assess actions and to develop and test new ideas facilitate behavioral change.
- Learning is more effective when it takes place as a collaborative rather than an isolated activity and in a context relevant to the learner (p. 16).

Perusal of Chapters 3 through 9 in this book shows us reflective practice in operation. Mentors encourage beginning teachers to identify problems, observe, analyze, reconceptualize, and then take action. They do so in each of the cases, in one way or another. The first case sets the tone when Darby and Esteban engage in mutual "caring reflection and dialogue."

I began this foreword with a vignette, so let me end with a story, and thus remain true to the style used by Yendol-Hoppey and Dana. It's a story about Harvard Law School in which 175 eager, albeit anxious, first-year law students await their first professor in their first course.

A middle-aged, scholarly-looking gentleman dressed in a dapper suit enters the huge auditorium through one of the doors adjacent to the stage. As the professor approaches the podium, he peers out at his students and selects his victim.

"You," pointing to a male student in the rear of the auditorium, "state the facts in the case before you." Nervously and hurriedly, the 175 students read the case. The student selected by the professor offers no response. Once again, the professor repeats his request. The student again freezes. Again the request is made. "State the facts in the case before you." The student gives an inadequate answer.

The professor nonchalantly reaches into his pocket and takes out a dime and says, "Take this dime, call your mother [it's an old story!], and tell her to pick you up because you'll never become a lawyer." Shocked, yet thankful they weren't called upon, the 174 other students anxiously await the student's reaction. No response.

"You heard what I said. Take this dime and tell your mother to pick you up." The student rises and walks slowly towards the stage. Hushed silence pervades the auditorium. Suddenly the student stops, looks up, and shouts, "Sir, you are a bastard!" Without batting an eyelash, the professor looks up and says, "Go back to your seat; you're beginning to think like a lawyer."

The Reflective Educator's Guide to Mentoring is an invaluable resource because it helps readers begin to *think and act* as mentors. It adds much to the literature on mentorship and supervision.

REFERENCES

Fosnot, C. T. (1989). *Enquiring teachers, enquiring learners: A constructivist approach to teaching.* New York: Teachers College Press.

Osterman, K. F., & Kottkamp, R. B. (2004). *Reflective practice for educators: Professional development to improve student learning* (2nd ed.). Thousand Oaks, CA: Corwin Press.

Sullivan, S., & Glanz, J. (2006). *Supervision that improves teaching: Strategies and techniques* (2nd ed.). Thousand Oaks, CA: Corwin Press.

Vygotsky, L. (2002). Vygotsky Resources. Retrieved August 31, 2006, from http://www.kolar.org/vygotsky/

Preface

The number of new teachers our nation will need in the next decade is astounding! In the next ten years, an anticipated two million new teachers will enter the teaching workforce (U.S. Department of Education, 1999). Although these teachers vary in their backgrounds as well as their pathways to teaching, they will all share the same need. Someone will need to provide them with support and guidance as they learn to teach. The question becomes who, and how?

Mentors have the power to shape the next generation of teachers. Their roles assume many varieties and flavors—some mentors work in partnership with a university, hosting semester-long student teachers or professional development school full-year interns in their classrooms. Some mentors are classroom teachers assigned the extra duty of serving as a mentor for one or more beginning teachers at their school. Some mentors are retired educators hired part-time by a district to mentor a number of novices in different schools. Some mentors are teachers who share their classrooms with a paid apprentice for one school year, at which time the apprentice "graduates" from apprenticeship and takes on his or her own classroom the following year. Particularly in schools with high teacher turnover and large numbers of alternatively prepared, uncertified teachers, some mentors are former classroom teachers released from their work in the classroom to full-time mentor a cohort of new teachers in one school building. Whatever type of mentor you are, one thing is certain—the work of mentoring is the most critical factor influencing who the next generation of teachers will become!

Having the awesome responsibility of shaping the knowledge, skills, and dispositions of the teachers who will be teaching your children, your grandchildren, and perhaps even your great-grandchildren can be both a joy and a challenge. Mentors find joy in their work as they feel that it is through mentoring novices that they can give back to the profession to which they committed their lives. Through mentoring, they often become professionally renewed, and new life is breathed into their own careers through the optimism, enthusiasm, eagerness, growth, or passion of the novices with whom they work. Mentors often feel professionally challenged in their work because mentoring involves simultaneously paying attention to a whole host of factors associated with learning to teach and reflection on one's own teaching, as well as a good deal of problem solving.

We wrote this book to recognize the power that mentors possess in shaping the work of novices who are learning to teach. Within the book, mentors who work with novice teachers share the metaphors that guide their work to help you deepen your understanding of effective mentoring; dissect the many discrete components that constitute effective mentoring; explore a variety of contexts and mentoring models; and, finally, reflect, learn, and grow in your own practice as mentor teachers.

This book emerges from our understanding of the professional development, mentoring, professional knowledge, and supervision literature as well as our own research on mentoring and learning to teach (see, for example, Dana & Silva, 2002; Silva & Dana, 2001; Silva & Tom, 2001; Yendol-Hoppey, in press; Yendol-Hoppey & Dana, 2006; Yendol-Silva & Dana, 2004), our own experiences serving in the role of mentor teacher, and our collective experience working with hundreds of educators serving in the role of mentor in various capacities since the mid-1980s. What we have learned from these mentor teachers and captured in the pages of this book is testament to all teachers who have chosen to support the needs of novices. Mentors are educators who truly recognize the power effective mentoring holds for transforming classrooms and schools to places where all children, and all teachers, can learn! Your work should be both shared and celebrated!

ABOUT THIS BOOK

Enlisting the help of story and metaphor, in this book we explore mentoring from many different angles. We begin in Chapter 1 by recognizing the need for skill-based mentor development as well as the importance of deep reflection on one's own mentoring practice. Both approaches are necessary for developing a rich mentoring practice that acknowledges the multifaceted nature of veteran teacher work with novice teachers. The voices of the mentors whose stories are captured in this book assert that their mentoring is indeed a reflective activity that is just as complicated as teaching. They argue that mentoring requires planned, intentional reflection on their years of experience as a thoughtful teacher. In Chapter 2, we tease apart the multiple components that mentoring entails by looking microscopically at what constitutes an effective mentor and three discrete entities of an effective mentor's work with the novice—creating the mentoring context, guiding a mentee's professional knowledge development, and cultivating the dispositions of a successful educator. This chapter sets the stage for mentors to contemplate how they can draw on existing strengths in their mentoring to prompt even more novice teacher professional knowledge and dispositional growth.

Next, in Chapters 3 through 9, the reader is introduced to seven different mentors and their work with mentees. Each mentor demonstrates different components of effective mentoring, and each mentor is presented using a different metaphor to frame, understand, and explore their mentoring practice. In Chapter 3 you meet Darby, a middle school teacher whose work with a student teacher, Juan, is captured by the metaphor of story-weaver. The story-weaver metaphor provides a vision of how one teacher took the time to get to know her intern and use the novice teacher's background as a starting point for developing his teaching skills. In Chapter 4, a fourth-grade classroom teacher, Kevin, is assigned to mentor four new teachers in his building. Like a jigsaw puzzle enthusiast, he figures out what the missing pieces are in each mentee's teaching practice and develops a sequence for helping novices find the missing pieces to their learning-to-teach puzzle. Chapter 5 introduces Robin, whose work with a yearlong intern resembles the careful work of a tailor, adjusting the novice's roles and responsibilities in the classroom based on her level of readiness and scaffolding the novice's thinking by tailoring specific probing questions to prompt planning. Tracy, the mentor portrayed in Chapter 6, works with her paid apprentice using the metaphor of coach, progressing through reflective coaching cycles with her mentee throughout the school year. Chapter 7 depicts mentor teacher, Claudia, as a "mirror" whose professional development school work with interns is characterized by the actions she takes to foster novice reflection. Chapters 8 and 9 portray urban high school mentors, Paige and Wesley, respectively. Paige's mentoring work as a retired educator hired part-time to mentor novices resembles the work of an interior designer, while Wesley's mentoring work as a classroom teacher released from his duties to mentor a cohort of new, alternatively certified teaching candidates at his high school resembles the work of a real estate agent.

Each mentor's metaphor and story is based on (and in many cases is written and contributed to this text by) a real mentor teacher who has lived the mentoring experience. According to Kenyon and Randall (1997), "To be a person is to have a story. More than that, it is to be a story" (p. 1). In our case, to be a mentor is to have a story. More than that, in Chapters 3 through 9 of this text, it is to *be* a story. The stories and metaphors of these mentors serve to help you develop your own identity as an effective mentor teacher, your own effective mentor story. Whatever your mentoring context, you will find yourself and your own unique mentoring makeup within each one of these metaphors. Exercises at the end of Chapters 1 and 2, as well as discussion questions at the end of Chapters 3 through 9, help you reflect on your mentoring practice, and learn and grow as a mentor teacher.

Finally, in Chapter 10, we name and summarize some of the tools that can be used to effectively mentor novice teachers. In addition, we provide specific ways for you to find support as you develop your mentoring practice. Finally, we suggest ways to continue reflecting on your practice as you continue to learn and grow as a mentor teacher.

WHO IS THIS BOOK FOR?

This book is for mentors who have already created a strong toolbox of "the nuts and bolts" of mentoring to help them deepen their mentoring practice. This book includes lessons learned from mentors across contexts—from the traditional mentor teacher who is working with a university preservice teacher entering the profession to the mentor teacher assigned a cohort of first-year alternatively certified teachers to support through their first years of teaching in a single school or district. This book is for mentors who might want to individually or collectively engage in a book study targeting deepening their practice. This book is for staff developers who train mentors in their districts, providing a multitude of ideas and discussion material for workshops on mentoring. This book is for university professors who conduct research on or teach classes on mentoring, providing the stimulus for serious discussion about the current state of mentoring by putting mentoring theory into practice, and mentoring practice into theory. This book is for university supervisors, field placement directors, and professional development school coordinators who wish to deepen their work with mentor teachers, creating richer and more powerful field experiences for their preservice students. Finally, this book is for principals who have hired novice teachers and want to ensure their success by assigning them a strong, effective mentor.

HOW TO USE THIS BOOK

This book serves as a stimulus for readers to engage in planned, thoughtful reflection on the ways years of experience as an effective classroom teacher can be translated efficiently and effectively to the next generation of teachers. If you are a mentor teacher, we suggest you go through this text chapter by chapter, engaging in the exercises at the end of Chapters 1, 2, and 10 and carefully considering the discussion questions at the end of Chapters 3 to 9. You may either engage in discussion of these questions with colleagues, or reflect individually on each mentor teacher portrayed in this book. In this way, we believe you will deepen your understanding of mentoring, heighten the visibility and the utility of the intrinsic mentoring tools you have already used or can adapt from your own experiences as a teacher, develop new tools for mentoring, and discover the unique mentor identity that resides within you.

If you are a staff developer, you can pair this text with a mentoring skill development text as you train mentor teachers within your district. By adding this text to your mentor development efforts, mentors begin to see how a mentoring practice becomes actualized. Each chapter can be read prior to a day of training, and the exercises can be completed and shared as part of your workshop and instruction on mentoring. You might also engage in a cooperative learning jigsaw activity during a part of your mentor training, where, after reading and discussing Chapters 1 and 2, individual mentors are assigned different metaphors (Chapters 3 to 9) to read and subsequently present to the entire group for discussion. Alternatively, you might review the content of Chapters 1, 2, and 10 at your beginning of the school year mentor training, and discuss Chapters 3 to 9 as a "warm-up" activity at subsequent mentor teacher meetings you hold for the district throughout the school year.

If you are a university professor who conducts research or teaches classes on mentoring, your students could discuss and debate the strengths and limitations of each approach to mentoring portrayed in this text. Doctoral students might benefit from an exercise in qualitative research where they look at Chapters 3 through 7 as data, and conduct a cross-case analysis, naming themes and patterns present across all of the mentor's work found in this book.

If you are a university supervisor, field placement director, or professional development school coordinator, you might read and discuss this text with your peers, gaining insights into new approaches to clinical education training provided for classroom teachers who host preservice teachers from your university. You might start a mentor study group in the schools you work in, meeting monthly with the mentor teachers at the building to discuss and engage in the exercises presented in this text, and deepen and expand your mentor teachers' interactions with preservice teacher education students from your institution.

Finally, if you are a principal, using this book, you could create and lead a study group of mentor teachers in your building as you collaboratively work to support the novices in your building. In so doing, you provide support for your veteran teachers who have taken on the additional responsibility of mentoring, as they engage in both the hard work of teaching and the hard work of mentoring another to teach!

However you use this book, we hope it will provide much "food for thought" in relationship to the complex process of mentoring, as well as the complex process of learning to teach. . . . Bon appetit!

Acknowledgments

We have been tremendously fortunate to have met and worked closely with a large number of extremely dedicated and talented educators who have chosen to give back to the profession of teaching by mentoring novice teachers. These dedicated professionals have not only unselfishly opened up their personal and professional lives to new teachers, but unselfishly opened up their personal and professional lives to us as we worked together to reform teacher education. These mentors have an understanding of mentoring as well as engage in research related to what it takes to learn to teach in reform-minded ways and, subsequently, to mentor teachers into the profession so they can survive in the existing system, understand how to be successful in the classroom, and join other teacher leaders working for educational change.

We are grateful to all of the mentor teachers at Alachua Elementary School and P. K. Yonge Developmental Research School who participate in the School Board of Alachua County–University of Florida Professional Development Community Program, and all of the mentor teachers we have worked with in the State College Area School District–Pennsylvania State University Elementary Professional Development School Program. In addition, we thank the mentor teachers in the Baltimore City Public School Mentoring Program and Duval County Public Schools (especially Helen Atkinson, Monica McAleer, and Melissa Dunn, our liaisons to these districts' mentors). The professional lives all of these teachers have touched through their mentoring are countless, and they have indeed impacted the future of teaching in immeasurable ways. We thank them all for their support of our learning about mentoring.

In particular, we wish to thank the mentor teachers and researchers who contributed core concepts to this book:

- Darby Claire Delane: Chapter 3: Mentor as Story-Weaver
- Kevin Berry: Chapter 4: Mentor as Jigsaw Puzzle Enthusiast
- Jennifer Jacobs: Chapter 5: Mentor as Tailor
- Tracy Norman: Chapter 6: Mentor as Coach
- Angela Gregory: Chapter 8: Mentor as Interior Designer

Without you, Darby, Kevin, Jennifer, Tracy, and Angela, this book would not have been possible!

We are indeed fortunate to have our professional and personal lives intertwine with one another in that our closest colleagues also happen to be our husbands. We wish to thank David Hoppey, Inclusion Specialist for Alachua County Schools, for continuing to push our thinking about issues of equity in education, and Tom Dana, Professor and Director of the School of Teaching and Learning at the University of Florida, for supporting innovative ways of working with schools, new teachers, and mentor teachers. We thank David and Tom for the numerous conversations we had as this book was unfolding, for their love, and for their support!

A supportive family is crucial to being able to get a book written. In addition to our husbands, we wish to thank our children, Caran, Billy, Kevin, Greg, and Kirsten for unselfishly giving up "Mom time" whenever we needed to write. In addition to our children, we thank our parents, Maureen and Bob Dunham and Ken and Anita Fichtman, who served as our life mentors, and whose unconditional love and support throughout our lifetimes enabled our writing to happen.

In addition to the abundant professional and personal support that is necessary to write a book, authors also need a space to get their writing done. Much of this book was written on a retreat. For sharing their condo with us so we could get the bulk of our writing completed away from the distractions of home and the office, we thank David and Cheryl Gregory. Finally, thanks to University of Florida's Center for School Improvement Senior Secretary Susan Stabel; University of Florida's College of Education Graphic Artist, Juawon Scott; and Corwin Press's Acquisitions Editor Faye Zucker for their respective work on formatting the manuscript, designing incredible figures to summarize major points in the text, and helping us tie all the loose ends together to get this book published!

Corwin Press gratefully acknowledges the contributions of the following reviewers:

Tom Ganser
Director
Office of Field Experiences
University of Wisconsin–Whitewater

Hal Portner
Educational Consultant
Florence, MA

Deb Pitton
Associate Professor of Education
Gustavus Adolphus College
St. Peter, MN

About the Authors

Diane Yendol-Hoppey is currently an Assistant Professor in the School of Teaching and Learning at the University of Florida. She spent the first fourteen years of her career in education teaching in a variety of public schools in Pennsylvania and Maryland. During her career as a classroom teacher, she served as a mentor teacher for both prospective and practicing teachers. In 1999, Diane received her PhD in curriculum and instruction from the Pennsylvania State University with an emphasis on teacher supervision. Since then, Diane has worked with mentor teachers within professional development schools and led the documentation of multiple mentoring and induction programs designed for both traditional and lateral-entry teachers within large urban school districts. Diane has contributed numerous articles to professional journals focused on mentoring, teacher leadership, professional development schools, and teacher inquiry.

Nancy Fichtman Dana is Professor of Education and Director of the Center for School Improvement at the University of Florida. She began her career in education as an elementary school teacher in Hannibal Central Schools, New York, where she first served in the role of mentor teacher for preservice students from State University of New York at Oswego. She received her PhD in elementary education from Florida State University. She has worked with classroom teachers in Florida and Pennsylvania to create powerful teacher education contexts, with particular attention to the role mentor teachers play in the learning-to-teach process. With Diane, she is author of

The Reflective Educator's Guide to Classroom Research, as well as numerous articles in professional journals focused on teacher inquiry, teacher leadership, school-university collaborations, and professional development schools.

Reflecting on Your Mentoring Practice

The Story of My Mother's Gravy

Mentors and apprentices are partners in an ancient human dance, and one of teaching's greatest rewards is the daily chance it gives us to get back on the dance floor. It is the dance of the spiraling generations in which the old empower the young with their experience and the young empower the old with new life, reweaving the fabric of the human community as they touch and turn.

—Palmer (1998, p. 25)

Congratulations! Whether you are supporting a first-year teacher in your district, have accepted the responsibility to partner with a university to promote the growth and development of a student teacher, or just have a general passion for advancing the professional growth of teaching colleagues, you are a participant in the ancient human dance described so eloquently by Parker Palmer—mentoring. Congratulations are in order, as the act of mentoring generates tremendous potential for teachers to be renewed professionally. The fatigue and burnout many teachers feel after numerous years in the profession are replaced with a renewed energy for their chosen field. Mentoring is perhaps the single most important act a veteran teacher can engage in to contribute to the future of the teaching profession.

WHY IS MENTORING SO IMPORTANT?

Let's look closely at some of the logistical variables that heighten the importance of mentoring. First, as a result of demographic trends related to increased student enrollments, teacher retirements, class size reduction, and teacher attrition, an increasing demand exists for public school teachers across our nation. An anticipated two million new teachers will enter the profession within the next decade (U.S. Department of Education, 1999). Florida alone needs 30,000 teachers a year and the colleges of education within Florida are only able to provide about 5,000, leaving a need for 25,000 new teachers. Like many states, Florida is developing alternative pathways to teaching, and as a result, many novices are arriving in their first classroom with limited pedagogical preparation.

Recruiting new teachers to fill these positions is critical, but even more critical is keeping new teacher recruits in the classroom. Statistics on teacher retention are grim—researchers have consistently found that younger teachers have high rates of departure (Ingersoll, 2001). In fact, several organizations, such as the National Commission on Teaching and America's Future, report, "with the exception of a few disciplines in specific fields, the nation graduates more than enough new teachers to meet its need each year. But after just three years, it is estimated that almost a third of new entrants to teaching have left the field, and after five years almost half are gone (National Commission on Teaching and America's Future, 2003, p. 19). In more challenging contexts, both rural areas and inner cities, these rates are often dramatically higher. Effective mentoring is an essential answer to the daunting attrition-rate problem (Feiman-Nemser, 1996). We need strong mentor teachers, and we need them fast!

Because the need for new teachers is so great, alternative entries to teaching accompanied by mentoring programs have sprouted up across the nation to augment the more traditional university student teacher or full-year internship teacher preparation model. In our work with mentoring, we have witnessed several different mentoring approaches that support traditionally and alternatively prepared teachers, including the following:

- Retired Educators—Mentors are retired teachers and administrators hired by a district to serve as part-time mentors of new inductees. Typically, these retired educators are less familiar with the school context, curriculum, and students within the classroom, but have numerous years of teaching experience to draw upon as they help others learn to teach.
- Cooperating Teachers—Mentors are classroom teachers who host a university student in their classroom for a single-semester student-teaching experience. Typically, these mentors view their role as providing a context for the novice to learn to teach and consider the onus of the responsibility for the new teacher's success as that of the university teacher education program.
- Yearlong Internship—Mentors are classroom teachers who coteach within their classroom with a yearlong intern from a university. These yearlong internships often unfold within professional development schools, where the mentor conceives of himself or herself as a school-based teacher educator.
- Apprenticeship Model—Mentors are classroom teachers who coteach with an alternatively certified teaching candidate. The teaching candidate, or *apprentice*, is paid as a paraprofessional during the apprenticeship year and assumes his or her own classroom the following school year.

- School-Based Mentor—Mentors are typically peers who have their own classrooms within the same school and assume the extra responsibility of mentoring a novice. This person may or may not have experience in the same grade level or subject matter as the novice and typically receives a small stipend.
- Full-Time Cohort Mentor—Mentors are responsible for supporting a cohort of new teachers placed within a single school. This model typically emerges in schools with high teacher turnover and large numbers of alternatively prepared, uncertified teachers. This mentor typically becomes a full-time member of the school faculty and becomes intimately familiar with the students, curriculum, and resources in the school and community.

The model within which you find yourself mentoring has implications for the types of support your mentee will need. For example, you may be mentoring preservice teachers in an undergraduate- or graduate-level teacher education program with relatively little classroom experience. You may be mentoring new teachers in your school who are engaged in the induction phase of their career and who are graduates of traditional teacher education programs and have completed a student teaching or internship experience. You may be mentoring new inductees at your school who increasingly arrive through alternative routes to teaching as they transition from a wide range of other careers, including the military, accounting, social work, and others.

In addition to these varied entry routes to teaching, novice teachers vary tremendously in age, life experiences, culture, race, language, and ability. They each bring to their teaching career teaching knowledge gained through their own experiences in K–12 education. Some of their experiences may be quite consistent with research-based teaching practice; however, the majority of these new teachers may possess beliefs that run counter to what is currently known about powerful instructional practice.

This immense variability in who is being mentored heightens the need for strong mentor teachers who possess a sensitivity to differentiating mentoring practice based on their mentee's background, life experiences, and needs. Mentors need to individualize for *every* new teacher, and each individual mentor teacher will need to carefully consider how he or she will facilitate the novice teacher's development. Figure 1.1 presents the logistical factors that contribute to the need to individualize for every mentee, illustrating the complexity of mentoring. As a result of this need for differentiation, tremendous responsibility is placed on your shoulders to support the success and survival of both the novice teacher you are mentoring and the children who learn within the novice's classroom. Remember, the *survival* of the novice teacher refers to whether they are able to navigate the complexity of the work life of a teacher within a bureaucratic system. The *success* of the novice teacher connects to the novice's ability to help children *learn*. Mentoring requires your attention to both survival and success.

In addition to the distinction made between novice teacher success and survival, who you are as a mentor teacher and who your mentee becomes as a classroom teacher is also dependent on your school context. Are you mentoring in a rural, urban, or suburban community? What is the socioeconomic status of the students in the school you serve? Are you teaching in an elementary, middle, or high school, and is that school public, private, religious, or charter? The logistical variables alone that surround mentoring serve to heighten the importance of quality mentoring! Regardless of who you are mentoring, or in what context you are mentoring them, this book is designed to help

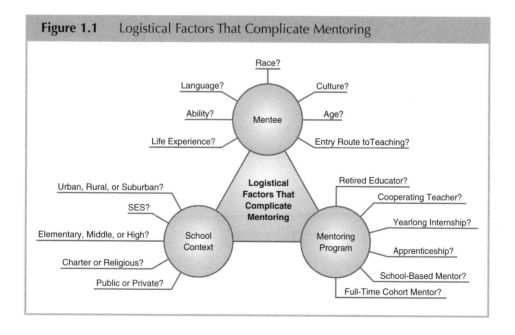

Figure 1.1 Logistical Factors That Complicate Mentoring

you visualize your role as mentor, differentiate for each mentee you work with, and enhance the mentoring skills you already possess and enact each day in your work with novice teachers.

HOW DO YOU ENHANCE YOUR MENTORING SKILLS?

Mentoring requires planned, intentional reflection on the ways years of experience as a thoughtful, reflective, reform-minded teacher can be captured and translated effectively to the next generation of teachers. We define *reform-minded* as a progressive stance toward teaching that acknowledges the importance of research-based practices, problematizing teaching and learning, and embracing change with the aim of educating all children. The goal of mentoring must be to cultivate these reform-minded practices in the novices who are entering the profession.

In the past decade, there has been a heightened interest in mentoring. Similarly, teacher education reformers "regard the mentor-novice relationship in the context of teaching as one of the most important strategies to support novices' learning to teach and, thus, to improve the quality of teaching" (Wang, 2001, p. 52). The importance and the heightened interest in mentoring as well as the increasing and pressing need for quality mentors has bred a number of manuals, guidebooks, and workshops on mentoring that identify the basic technical skills necessary for effective mentoring. Texts such as Hal Portner's *Mentoring New Teachers* (2003), and Hicks, Glasgow, and McNary's *What Successful Mentors Do* (2005) are excellent resources that help mentors develop the foundation for working skillfully with novice teachers. However, in addition to understanding the technical skills that provide the foundation for the act of mentoring, it is also important to reflect on the ways these skills play out with different novices and in different contexts.

WHY IS IT IMPORTANT TO BE REFLECTIVE ABOUT ONE'S MENTORING?

On the surface, this may appear to be a silly question. After all, it would seem that with numerous years of teaching experience under your belt, mentoring would be a natural process that would just happen as a result of sharing the same classroom and children with a student teacher, or in serving as a buddy for a novice teacher, answering questions and sharing district and school procedures to help him or her through his or her first few years of teaching. Yet, research tells us that outstanding teaching does not readily and intuitively translate to outstanding mentoring. For example, in an extensive research study comparing mentor teachers in the United States, United Kingdom, and China, Wang (2001) found that

> Relevant teaching experience, though important, is not a sufficient condition for a teacher to be a professional mentor. Mentors who are practicing or moving toward practicing the reform-minded teaching may not develop the necessary conceptions and practices of mentoring that offer all the crucial opportunities for novices to learn to teach in a similar way. Thus, when selecting mentor teachers, not only is it important to consider the relevant teaching experiences of mentors but it is also important to identify how mentors conceptualize mentoring and their relevant experience in conducting the kind of mentoring practices expected. (pp. 71–72)

Identifying how you conceptualize mentoring, therefore, is a critical process that can only happen as a result of reflecting deeply on mentoring. Teaching novices to teach can be extremely rewarding, but extremely complex as well. Consider the summary Wang (2001) provides of the needs of novice teachers:

> Research suggests that to learn to teach for understanding, novice teachers need opportunities to form a strong commitment toward reform-minded teaching (Cochran-Smith & Lytle, 1999) and to develop a deeper understanding of subject matter (Ball & McDiarmid, 1989). They need opportunities to learn how to represent what they teach effectively in classrooms (Shulman, 1987) and how to connect what they teach to students with different backgrounds (Kennedy, 1991). They also need opportunities to learn how to conduct the kind of reflection that supports their continuous learning to teach (Schön, 1987, p. 69)

Because the needs of the novice are many, and each novice is different, there is no single way to mentor that will work with every novice in every context in the same way. Mentors need to reflect on their skills and make decisions about which basic mentoring skills must be invoked with each novice in each context at different times and for different purposes throughout the mentoring process. Becoming reflective about your mentoring and developing your own unique mentoring identity through the reflective process deepens your ability to influence the novice teacher. Becoming reflective about your mentoring recognizes the unique challenges individuals learning to teach face, and raises your voice in discussions of reform-minded teaching. Through becoming reflective about your mentoring, you contribute to the grand professional conversation about the future of education in this country. You breathe new life into your own career, you breathe new life into the teaching profession itself, and you breathe new life into the education of children across the nation.

One way to reflect on mentoring is through deep examination of who one is as a teacher, and the ways one's teaching identity translates into the development of a unique and effective identity as a mentor (Ganser, 1998). In our work with mentors, we have found the use of metaphors to be a powerful venue to generate deep examination of one's identity as a mentor. More than two decades ago, George Lakoff and Mark Johnson helped us to think in a whole new way about the language that we use, as they asserted in their book *Metaphors We Live By* that metaphor is much more than mere poetical and rhetorical embellishments. According to these authors,

> Metaphor is pervasive in everyday life, not just in language but in thought and action. Our ordinary conceptual system, in terms of which we both think and act, is fundamentally metaphorical in nature. (Lakoff & Johnson, 1980, p. 3)

Similarly, Parker Palmer asserts that good talk about good teaching and the identity from which good teaching comes can occur through the exploration of metaphors and images that can enrich a teacher's sense of the self who teaches (Palmer, 1998). Parallel to Parker's line of logic, we believe exploring metaphors of mentoring can generate good talk about good mentoring and enrich a mentor's sense of self as both teacher of children and teacher of teachers.

Hence, the purpose of this book is to help readers reflect deeply on the act of mentoring and find their own identity as a mentor teacher through the examination of different stories and metaphors used by accomplished teachers to guide their mentoring practice. Each chapter describes the case of a mentor teacher and his or her interactions with the protégé with whom he or she works. Following the text of each chapter is a series of questions carefully crafted to facilitate rich conversation among colleagues about mentoring. By reading about the lives of mentor teachers who conceptualize the mentoring role in varying ways, as well as engaging in dialogue with teaching colleagues to tease apart the inherent complexities of mentoring evident in each metaphor presented in this book, we hope you will gain unique and rich insights into your own life as a teacher and mentor. To exemplify this process, we end this chapter with a story written by Bobby Ann Starnes (2001). The story depicts the process a daughter goes through as she longs for her mother to teach her how to make gravy.

Last Thanksgiving, I tried to make my mother's gravy. As always, I failed miserably. Standing at the stove stirring the mixture, getting it wrong again, I had a vivid image of the day I asked my mother to teach me.

She seemed puzzled, as though she thought the ability to make gravy should have been transmitted genetically. She could not recall anyone teaching her. Almost reluctantly, she agreed. So I stood by her side at the old Kelvinator range in our small kitchen, pencil and paper in hand, ready to record every detail.

She began with the same cast-iron skillet she had used every morning for as long as I could remember. "You put the drippings in the pan," she said, turning the burner to medium high. I quickly wrote "medium high" on my paper. My mother looked at me in disbelief.

"How much?" I asked, anxious to get down every step and detail.

"Oh, just some," she replied, spreading the goods evenly over the skillet surface. Just some, I thought. Just some!

"Now, mix the flour in," she said, pulling her cup out of the Gold Medal bag.

"How much?"

"Enough," she said in an impatient tone. "You put enough flour in to get the right thickness."

Well, yes, I thought. You'd certainly want to use enough. It wouldn't make sense to use too much or too little. But how much is enough? I was still trying to figure out what to write, when, at what seemed a completely arbitrary moment, she said, "Now

(Continued)

(Continued)

a pinch of salt…a dash of pepper." I wondered how to convert "a pinch" into teaspoons and what the difference between a pinch and a dash might be.

She mixed the ingredients until the paste reached the right consistency—a consistency only she seemed able to detect. Then she added milk, whipped the spoon around a little, and voila, perfect gravy.

Mother never used a recipe, and she laughed lightly when I suggested she write one out for me. My mother understood gravy. She just knew how much of this or that she needed—salt, pepper, milk, and butter in quantities of a pinch, a dash, a handful. She knew how to thicken or thin, how to get it just brown enough. She knew how the ingredients interacted. And by watching carefully, she knew when to add each. She could see a problem before it occurred, and she knew how to head it off. She paid attention, and even when she seemed distracted by the potatoes or the bread or crying children, she kept it all in her head and responded to each situation at just the right moment. I don't remember things ever burning or a time when all the food didn't reach the table at the same time—hot foods hot, cold foods cold. No matter how complex the meal or how numerous the distractions, she could focus on everything at once and pick up the signals that prompted her to act.

After last Thanksgiving's failure, I finally gave up on ever being able to make my mother's gravy. Instead, I decided to make my own. Dumping the food into the sink, I smiled as I remembered myself anxiously trying to copy her every movement exactly. I can't make hers, I thought, but she taught me a lot about gravy. As a result, I learned to make my gravy. And it is good. (Starnes, 2001)

Similar to the daughter in this parable, this book requires you to reject the notion that there is a perfect or simple recipe for effective mentoring. Rather, you have the power to *understand mentoring* by discovering the unique, effective form of mentoring that lies within you by carefully and critically scrutinizing the ways seven teachers metaphorically conceptualize their roles as mentors. For, as Parker Palmer asserts, "Good teaching cannot be reduced to technique: good teaching comes from the identity and integrity of the teacher" (1998, p. 10). Similarly, good mentoring cannot be reduced to technique: It comes from the identity, integrity, and understanding of the mentor.

While there is no one recipe for mentoring, we do know a good deal about the individual components that formulate the knowledge base for mentoring. Therefore, in Chapter 2, we examine mentoring by defining effective mentoring and looking at each discrete component of the effective mentoring process—creating an educative mentoring context, guiding a mentee's professional knowledge development, and nurturing the development of a mentee's professional dispositions.

Next, in Chapters 3 through 8, you will meet seven effective mentor teachers, and get glimpses into their mentoring practices through the metaphor they utilize to conceptualize mentoring—Darby, a storyweaver; Kevin, a jigsaw puzzle enthusiast; Robin, a tailor; Tracy, a coach; Claudia, a mirror; Paige, an interior designer; and Wesley, a real estate agent. Although you cannot become Darby, Kevin, Robin, Tracy, Claudia, Paige, or Wesley, these teachers can teach you a lot about mentoring.

At the close of each chapter, you may deepen your understanding of mentoring as you further explore each teacher's mentoring identity and integrity through careful deliberation and discussion of the chapter questions raised to help generate insights into the shadows and strengths each metaphor reveals, as well as the ingredients each mentor used to create his or her own unique approach to mentoring. In discussion of the metaphors with others, you may also discover the guidance mentoring metaphors may offer during the more difficult and arduous times of teaching another to teach. Rooted in an image that arises from somewhere in our psyche, metaphor can save us from the quick technical fix we always long for when we examine the complicated process of teaching and teaching others to teach.

As a result of this text, we hope you will be well on your way to making your own mentoring gravy . . . and we know that it will be good!

Chapter 1 Exercises

To foster deep reflection on mentoring, it is critical to take an inventory of who you are professionally and what you currently believe about mentoring. These exercises are designed to foster this process.

1. Create a mentoring platform (similar to a political platform that shares one's espoused beliefs). To create this platform, brainstorm a bulleted list that represents your beliefs about what effective mentoring is. Begin your bulleted list with the statement, "I believe effective mentoring is . . . "

2. Which components of this bulleted list are the most challenging to enact as a mentor? Which are the easiest to enact as you mentor?

(Continued)

(Continued)

3. Write your own autobiography of mentoring by reflecting on your experiences learning to teach and your first few years of teaching. Name the most critical incidents in your own learning-to-teach process. What role did mentoring play in these critical incidents? How do your own experiences learning to teach translate into your own philosophy of mentoring? Discuss how you came to hold the beliefs you described in your mentoring platform.

4. Create a time line of people who influenced your life as a professional. Describe how each one contributed to your learning.

5. Follow the guide provided below to design a "Mentor's Coat of Arms." In Space 1, draw a real or mythical animal that best describes the mentor you want to be. In Space 2, choose a real symbol, or create your own design, for an insignia that best describes the mentor you want to be. In Space 3, choose one color in any shade—or a rainbow effect—that best describes the mentor you want to be. In Space 4, draw one character, real or fictional, that best describes the mentor you want to be. In Space 5, choose one word that best describes the mentor you want to be. How you write that word should also help describe the mentor you want to be.

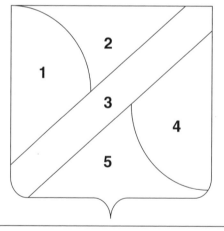

Exploring the Complexity of Mentoring

What It Takes to Be an Effective Mentor

In order to explore the complex nature of mentoring, we begin this chapter by revisiting a complexity you are already quite familiar with as a result of the years you have spent as a teacher—the inherently complex nature of the act of teaching itself! To illustrate, let's talk about what it means to be a teacher for a moment. Effective teachers must know their content deeply, know pedagogy, know human development, know the 25 (in elementary schools) to more than 100 (in secondary schools) students they interact with each day, including identifying each one of these learners' academic, social, and emotional needs, and teachers must attend to these 25 or so individuals' needs, all unique and varied, all at the same time during each instructional moment of the day. Teachers must understand lesson planning, and understand that with every lesson taught, there will be a unique outcome that results from the interaction of the context, the timing of the teaching, the teacher himself or herself, and the learners in the room. Teachers must attend to management and transitions of large groups of learners before, during, and after each lesson. Teachers are bombarded with decision making each minute of their day, ranging from deciding the next steps when a planned lesson is not progressing productively to deciding if Johnny, who just asked to use the bathroom for the third time that day, should be given permission to leave the lesson to take care of his personal needs. In addition, teachers must constantly formally and informally assess their students' learning and progress. Teachers make contributions to the running of the school, managing such tasks as the collection of lunch money, lunch counts, bus duties, and lunch duties. They must communicate and collaborate with parents and other education professionals such as guidance counselors, the principal, school psychologists, and other teaching colleagues. In their spare time, they serve on committees, attend faculty meetings, and read professional journals and books to keep abreast of the latest developments in their field. They do all this while simultaneously keeping an eye on high-stakes testing and their students' performance, balancing preparation for test taking and the teaching of test-taking skills with real teaching and learning of content.

This picture we've painted of a teacher's work is by no means complete, but we believe it is complete enough to illustrate what is meant by the inherently complex nature of teaching. Superimpose, upon all the variables just described that make teaching a complex act, the responsibility of teaching another person to teach. It is logical to deduce that the business of mentoring becomes even more complex than the business you have engaged in for years—teaching itself!

The purpose of this chapter is to untangle some of the complexities of mentoring by exploring the different components that constitute an effective mentor. Understanding the many ingredients or components that are a part of mentoring can help you honor the complexity that mentoring entails. During the past 30 years, researchers and educational theorists have studied the work of mentors, and the brief synthesis of the research that follows offers insight into the intricacies of your mentoring work. By eavesdropping on the research literature related to mentoring, you can jump-start your own thinking about mentoring and how you might both enact and expand your role.

Let's begin exploring the intricacies of mentoring by eavesdropping on two leading researchers in the field—Jian Wang and Sandra Odell (2002). According to Wang and Odell, any discussion about effective mentoring must begin with a discussion about effective teaching. In a seminal article titled "Mentored Learning to Teacher According to Standards-Based Reform: A Critical Review," Wang and Odell discuss the latest thinking on effective teaching. According to these scholars, the new curriculum and teaching standards regarding effective teaching in the United States consistently advocate a kind of teaching that is focused on conceptual understanding of subject matter, connections between learning and their pedagogical experiences in real-life contexts, active discovery of ideas, and careful examination of the ideas in a community of learners. This type of teaching is complex, and as a result, mentoring must be "educative."

Another leading scholar in the area of teacher mentoring, Sharen Feiman-Nemser (2001), introduced the idea of *educative mentoring* by building on Dewey's (1938) concept of educative experiences. Dewey identified educative experiences as those that promote rather than retard future growth and lead to richer subsequent experiences. Similarly, your mentoring work should promote future growth that leads to richer learning experiences for both the mentee and the students within the novice's classroom. Educative mentoring

> combines instructional, technical and emotional support with rich opportunities for mentor and beginning teachers to work collaboratively on authentic issues of development of high quality practice that impacts student learning. (Assist Beginning Teachers, n.d.)

Simply stated, effective mentoring must be *educative*.

Now that we have acknowledged the complexity of mentoring and committed to the goal of educative mentoring, we are ready to explore the many elements that compose the content of educative or effective mentoring. Educative mentoring is a complicated act, as it entails simultaneously attending to three components: creating an educative mentoring context, guiding a mentee's professional knowledge development, and cultivating the dispositions of a successful educator.

CREATING AN EDUCATIVE MENTORING CONTEXT

It is not uncommon for us to hear exhausted teachers lament, "If only I could just *teach,* my job would be so much simpler!" Good teachers understand that before teaching academic content can ever happen, they must work diligently to create a context within which their teaching can unfold. To accomplish this, teachers take time to do such things as understand and attend to students' social and emotional needs, develop relationships with their learners, and assess background knowledge and skills learners bring with them to a lesson. Similarly, if you could just *mentor,* mentoring would be so much simpler! Yet, good mentoring can only happen if you work diligently to create a context for your mentoring to unfold. There are three areas that are imperative to attend to when creating your mentoring context—providing emotional support, creating a strong relationship, and ascertaining the prior knowledge and beliefs about teaching your mentee brings into the classroom.

Providing Emotional Support

Not surprisingly, the theoretical and research-based literature in the area of teacher mentoring has long recognized the importance of providing psychological and emotional support to help novice teachers' entry into the profession, keep them there, and help them become successful educators (Gold, 1996; Huling-Austin, 1990). This work, rooted in humanistic psychology and the work of Carl Rodgers, remains important today as the current context of high-stakes accountability, low teacher pay, challenging students, emotional and psychological stress, low professional status, uncertainty in the classroom, and difficult working conditions make the attrition of novice teachers a never-ending concern. Given these challenges, a mentor must provide emotional support to the novice, and this emotional support is often an essential underpinning to any future professional development.

Creating a Strong Relationship

Creating a context for your mentoring to unfold would be complex even if your *only* job was to support the emotional needs of your mentee. However, attending to the professionally related emotional needs of your mentee is just the tip of creating an educative mentoring-context iceberg! To create an educative mentoring context, you must also develop a trusting and respectful working relationship. This relationship requires both the mentor and mentee to establish open lines of communication with one another, and be willing participants. Without the willing participation on the part of a novice, the mentor will have difficulty engaging in educative mentoring.

Decades of research exist indicating the central importance of a quality mentor-novice relationship as a necessity to promoting novice teacher learning. Related to developing trust and respect is the importance of both the mentor and the novice understanding the difference between mentoring and evaluating. Mentoring is about supporting novices learning to teach, and evaluation is about documenting performance for employment decision-making purposes. Mentors should not be involved in evaluating novices and should maintain a level of confidentiality that allows novices to trust the relationship and share concerns about their own teaching practice. A mentor's goal is really to do everything within his or her means to assure the mentee's success and survival as a classroom teacher. Last, but certainly not least, mentors need to recognize the issues of power inherent in their relationship with the novice teacher. A mentor needs to identify ways to encourage the novice to exercise agency rather than act as a passive recipient in the learning-to-teach process. Given the complexity of teaching, the mentee must be an active participant in the construction of the complex knowledge of teaching. Acknowledging the importance of developing a quality mentor-novice relationship will facilitate your ability to influence novice teacher growth, as will ascertaining the prior knowledge and beliefs about teaching your mentee brings into the classroom.

One way to deepen your relationship with your mentee is to garner a full understanding of the mentee's existing beliefs about teaching and learning. Research indicates that teachers' beliefs highly influence their decision making and, ultimately, their performance (Lortie, 1975). Given that novice teachers bring a host of beliefs to their teaching that formed as a result of their own K–12 education, mentors must uncover what these beliefs about teaching are throughout the mentoring process (Ball & McDiarmid, 1989). Without the mentor and mentee explicitly recognizing, acknowledging, and inquiring into these beliefs, it is difficult for substantial growth to occur.

One way that mentors often access a novice's beliefs is by helping the novice create a teaching platform (Nolan & Hoover, 2005; Sergiovanni & Starratt, 2002). A teaching platform articulates exactly what new teachers believe is powerful teaching by laying out their thoughts about the role of students, instruction, content knowledge, curriculum, the role of the teacher, and the influence of context. Some evidence suggests that mentoring should aim at naming, critiquing, shifting, and eventually increasing the correspondence between the novice's teaching platform and the novice's actual teaching (Franke & Dahlgren, 1996).

Although creating a ripe context for mentoring to take place is an essential component to educative mentoring, the knowledge base is much deeper. Once the context is created for a mentor and a novice to explore teaching, a mentor must attend to multiple areas of knowledge development.

GUIDING A MENTEE'S PROFESSIONAL KNOWLEDGE DEVELOPMENT

One of the aspects of teaching that makes it so complex is the multiple knowledge bases teachers draw upon simultaneously as they plan for instruction and make decisions about teaching. Intrigued with learning more about the complicated thought processes of good teachers, educational researchers have teased apart and named these multiple knowledge bases (see, for example, Good & Brophey, 1994; Levin & Nolan, 2000; Shulman, 1987). According to these scholars, the thinking that occurs during the act of teaching draws upon seven interrelated knowledge bases—content knowledge, pedagogical knowledge, student-learner knowledge, curriculum knowledge, pedagogical-content knowledge, context knowledge, and classroom-management knowledge. To engage in educative mentoring, it is critical to pay attention to mentees' knowledge development in each one of these areas so mentees can reach their fullest teaching potential.

Content Knowledge Development

Fairly or unfairly, teachers today are under attack as policymakers claim a lack of content knowledge in our teaching force. More important, a body of literature exists noting that teachers need a deeper understanding of what they need to teach in order for them to be effective instructional decision makers (Ball & McDiarmid, 1989). Educational researchers Deborah Ball and G. Williamson McDiarmid specify three aspects of content knowledge essential for teaching. First, the teacher must understand the central facts, concepts, theories, and procedures essential to the lesson content. Second, the teacher must have an explanatory framework that organizes and connects the ideas for both himself or herself and the students. Third, the teacher must understand the rules for evidence within the content area (Shulman, 1986). Often, mentors and novices do not realize that the source of a poor lesson may be the novices' lack of content knowledge. Thus, mentors need to help novices make the underpinnings of the content they are teaching explicit, and when novices need help identifying the content, mentors have a responsibility to support content knowledge development.

Pedagogical Knowledge Development

A second form of professional knowledge focuses on developing general pedagogical expertise, which begins by becoming familiar with instructional tools of the trade. Novice teachers need mentor support as they develop this repertoire of instructional tools including, but not limited to, familiarity with standards as well as the ability to plan, deliver, and assess meaningful learning experiences (Wasley, Hampel, & Clark, 1997). According to Feiman-Nemser (2001), "Good teachers know about a range of approaches to curriculum, instruction, and assessment; and they have the judgment, skill, and understanding to decide what to use when" (p. 1018). Although some novices enter the first teaching experiences with some familiarity with instructional tools related to planning, delivering, and assessing instruction, they will need help expanding and perfecting their use of these tools.

Student Learner Knowledge Development

Even when novices understand the content they are teaching and have a foundation in the process of planning, teaching, and assessing, they often don't have sufficient knowledge of the learners in their classroom. As a result, they struggle to design appropriate and differentiated instruction. If they do not know their learners or have background experiences with similar learners to draw on, instructional and curricular decision making becomes difficult. Novice teachers need to develop an understanding of child and adolescent development, including what students are able to do at various ages, if they are to develop appropriate learning activities. Beyond a general understanding of child and adolescent development, novices need to become familiar with the unique aspects of each student in their classroom. As a result, mentors need to help novices get to know their students both individually and collectively. This can be done as mentors help new teachers analyze student work, compare student success with various curricular materials, and interview students to better understand their thinking, as well as help novices observe the differing impact their instruction has on different students. Mentors can also facilitate this process by providing novices with opportunities to learn about their students (Ladson-Billings, 1999; Zeichner & Hoeft, 1996). This type of learner knowledge is essential as, without this understanding, a successful and differentiated lesson will be difficult to plan.

Curriculum Knowledge Development

Even when novice teachers have a strong understanding of the students in their classroom, they often have difficulty setting appropriate expectations and adjusting curriculum for students in their classrooms. The process of making those curricular adjustments requires an understanding of the curriculum standards for multiple subject areas, the organization of the curriculum, the sequence of the curriculum, and how to differentiate curriculum based on student needs. According to Feiman-Nemser (2001), the ambitious teaching that is represented in today's new curriculum frameworks and standards documents must be worked out by teachers themselves if they are to be able to enact the central tenets of the curriculum. Enacting the quality of curriculum advocated in the current standards set by professional organizations today will require mentors to work together with their mentee as they enact this educational change.

Helping novice teachers construct complex curriculum knowledge will require mentors to introduce curriculum standards, make explicit current research on curriculum implications for student learning, and help novices negotiate the element of high-stakes testing. These three influences on curriculum decision making simultaneously bombard new teacher thinking as they enter the profession and begin designing instruction. One dilemma is that many novices do not view knowledge, learning, and teaching in a manner consistent with standards-based reform, but, rather, their views reflect their own experiences in schools (Wang & Odell, 2002). Indeed, new teachers will need mentor support as they figure out how to teach for student conceptual understanding of the subject matter while still attending to the pressures of high-stakes accountability.

Pedagogical Content Knowledge Development

Although many educators don't use the term *pedagogical content knowledge* (PCK) as they share with others their practical knowledge of teaching, indeed, PCK is the most complex form of teacher knowledge. This knowledge is hard to pin down, as it requires the simultaneous integration of the many other forms of professional knowledge discussed. PCK is an elaborate name for the unique knowledge construction that occurs in a teachers' minds as they blend their knowledge of the context, content, instructional pedagogy, and their students (Grossman, 1990; Shulman, 1986, 1987). This type of teacher knowledge emerges as teachers think about how to connect a specific subject matter to students with diverse backgrounds and academic needs within a particular school characterized by limited resources and significant accountability pressures, while at the same time considering the potential misconceptions the students may hold. This is precisely the type of complex knowledge that makes "cookbook" approaches to teaching and mentoring inadequate. Mentors can help novices develop PCK by making their own thinking around these points explicit during the planning process. At times, this will require deepening subject matter understanding, helping novices think about academic content from the perspective of their students, and learning how to organize students to learn the content (Feiman-Nemser, 1990).

Context Knowledge Development

The importance of helping novice teachers understand the organization where they teach should not be underestimated. Figuring out the politics of schools on top of trying to meet the needs of 25 students within a classroom is often more than a novice teacher can handle independently. Novice teachers will need help understanding and negotiating the contexts where they teach if they are to survive within the system. For example, new teachers need to understand district policy, the principal's leadership style, the school's mission and vision, the roles and responsibilities of each educator in the building, and the community that surrounds the school. Additionally, novices need to gain access to the professional language and dialogue of the school, knowledge of resources available and who controls those resources, and the language of education reform. One other factor present in the schools is micropolitics. According to Blase (1991),

> Micropolitics refers to the use of formal and informal power by individuals and groups to achieve their goals in organizations. In large part, political actions result from perceived differences between individuals and groups, coupled with the motivation to use power to influence and/or protect. Although such actions are consciously motivated, any action, consciously or unconsciously motivated, may have political "significance" in a given situation. Both cooperative and conflictive actions and processes are part of the realm of micropolitics. (p. 11)

In today's context, this means that mentors need to support novices as they negotiate the micropolitics of their school and help them understand colleagues' use of power to influence or protect, to cooperate, or to engage in conflict.

Classroom Management Knowledge Development

Any experienced teacher recognizes the importance of standard routines and procedures as some of the most effective tools in maintaining classroom discipline. As a result, mentors need to help novices acquire a repertoire of standard routines and procedures to make sure students understand that there are expectations for behavior in their classroom. Knowledge of classroom management includes how students are expected to use classroom and school facilities and how to establish routines or procedures that make the day run smoothly. For example, novices must learn how to get students ready for the school day, how to organize the submission of student work, how to provide feedback, how to distribute resources, and how to establish expectations for student behavior. Thus, in addition to the previous six forms of professional knowledge shared, novices need explicit help in developing a knowledge base for classroom management.

Effective mentors would have a huge job ahead of them if their mentoring work entailed paying attention to a mentee's knowledge growth and development in a single area. One of the factors that clearly complicates mentoring is there isn't just one knowledge base, but at least seven that mentors must attend to! Attending to all areas has become increasingly important in recent years as more and more mentees enter the profession through alternative means, other than university teacher education programs. For example, if your mentee is from a university teacher education program, he or she at the least has a foundational book knowledge of pedagogical and classroom management tools and, through the university, has studied his or her content in depth. A mentee from an alternative entry route to teaching might enter with substantial content knowledge in mathematics but also as a pedagogically blank slate, having never considered or been introduced to pedagogical and classroom management tools. As if attending to mentee knowledge development in seven different areas wasn't complicated enough for you, we now add another layer to what it takes to be an effective mentor—attending to the development of your mentee's professional dispositions!

NURTURING THE DEVELOPMENT OF A MENTEE'S PROFESSIONAL DISPOSITIONS

As you drive on the road these days, it is not uncommon to see bumper stickers that hint at the identity of the driver in the vehicle. Stickers with sayings such as "Born to Shop" and "Born to Dance" adorn car bumpers. Similar to the drivers of these cars who advertise their passions, many outstanding educators (especially outstanding educators like yourselves, who wish to have a part in shaping the next generation of the teaching profession through mentoring) often feel that they are "born to teach." The notion of being born to teach has been captured by noted educational researcher William Ayers (1989).

In his study of six exemplary preschool teachers, he came to the conclusion that

> there is no clear line delineating the person and the teacher. Rather, there is a seamless web between teaching and being, between teacher and person. Teaching is not simply what one does, it is who one is. (p. 130)

When we recognize that teaching is not simply what one does, but who one is, it becomes critical to examine the professional dispositions that are a part of our mentee's makeup. Professional dispositions refer to a prevailing frame of mind or spirit that is part of the fabric of not just who one is as a teacher, but who one is as a person as well. In this section, we examine four professional dispositions that educative mentors help mentees discover and examine within themselves—a commitment to equity, a commitment to inquiry, a commitment to collaboration, and a commitment to a strong work ethic.

Commitment to Equity

By the year 2010, one-third of all children in the United States will be members of groups currently considered minorities, while the majority of teachers will remain White and female with little experience with those who are different from themselves (National Commission on Teaching and America's Future, 1996, 1997). Given the increasing diversity of schools (race, class, gender, language, culture, and ability) today and the fact that novices typically are assigned the lowest ability students and the most challenging classes (Kilgore, Ross, & Zbikowski, 1990; Rust, 1994), mentors have a responsibility to cultivate a commitment and stance toward teaching for equity. Many novice teachers arrive in their first positions with negative assumptions about diverse students, and they often lack confidence in their ability to reach students who are different from themselves.

According to Cochran-Smith (1991), cultivating a commitment to equity often requires developing a dissatisfaction with current teaching practice, recognizing that current teacher practice often deflates freedom, equality, and student dignity. The mentor's role requires helping the new teacher critically analyze current teaching practice. As a part of this critique, the mentors help mentees see their students in a new light and analyze classroom interactions in new and different ways that acknowledge who the students are and what they bring to the classroom (Achinstein & Barrett, 2004). By nurturing a commitment to equity in new teachers, the mentor helps them become agents of change and advocates for *all* students.

Commitment to Inquiry

As already discussed numerous times in this text, teaching is an inherently, incredibly complex endeavor. Because it is so complex, it is natural and normal for teachers to face many issues, tensions, problems, and dilemmas as they practice. Issues, tensions, problems, and dilemmas of practice continue to arise throughout the entire span of one's career as a teacher. Therefore, questioning one's own practice becomes a necessary and natural part of a teacher's and a mentor's work. Rather than "sweeping problems under the carpet" and pretending they don't exist, in order to continue to learn and grow professionally, teachers and mentors embrace problems by deliberately naming them, making them public, and making a commitment to do something about them. Doing something about problems of practice requires first understanding them in a systematic way. Hence, teachers study practice, becoming students of their own teaching. Engaging in teacher research (Dana & Yendol-Silva, 2003), lesson study (Watanabe, 2003), and critical friend groups (Bambino, 2002) are all ways teachers become students of their own teaching.

Educative mentors model what it means to be a student of one's own teaching for the novice. Oftentimes, this occurs by simply thinking out loud in front of the mentee as a mentor grapples with his or her own dilemma of practice. In addition, educative mentors are not afraid to push their mentee's thinking by purposefully creating dissonance in a mentee's teaching experience. Evidence suggests that a reasonable level of dissonance plays a powerful role in teacher learning (Elliott, 1991, 1997), as dissonance becomes a spring that propels the novice teacher into a space where learning can take place. Since dissonance can often cause discomfort, mentees must help the novice teacher recognize that dissonance is a powerful impetus for professional growth that should be embraced rather than smothered—it's okay for a mentee to pose difficult questions to the mentor, and it's okay for the mentor to pose difficult questions to the mentee! The posing and exploration of questions that cause dissonance deepens the development of a mentee's inquiring disposition.

Finally, mentors invite their mentees to engage in collaborative inquiry. A key part of a mentor's role in nurturing a mentee's commitment to inquiry is helping the mentee unearth a problem or dilemma of practice. Schön (1983) describes this as problem setting. The mentor and mentee interactively name the things they wish to collaboratively explore. In this way, mentors help novices become skilled in the type of reflection that facilitates continuous learning throughout the novice's professional lifetime (Schön, 1987).

Commitment to Collaboration

Teachers in today's school recognize the importance of teacher collaboration for improving schools (Darling-Hammond & McLaughlin, 1995; Fullan, 1993). Specifically, collaboration is critical if teachers seek to reach all students within their classroom (Brownell, Yeager, Rennells, & Riley, 1997; Friend & Cook, 1990). To address the needs of an increasingly diverse population, teachers must possess the sophisticated skills to support each other, facilitate learning, and problem solve together. The Holmes Group (1995) identified the importance of cultivating a "collective will" to help us address the needs of today's children and youth. Novice teachers need to learn how to collaborate within their work environment so that they can contribute to ongoing improvement in their professional practice. A mentor can help build the foundation for novices to collaborate with other professionals.

Commitment to a Strong Work Ethic

Those who have never taught may consider being a teacher because it's such an "easy life"—rather than working an 8:00 to 5:00 day, teachers "get off" somewhere around 3:00 p.m.! Those who teach can't help but laugh at this ridiculous characterization of their work. Teaching involves a workday that extends far beyond the time a teacher spends with kids. Teachers plan, assess, grade, communicate with parents, attend meetings to take part in school decision making, read professional literature, review content, and so on, and so on, and so on. Teachers are personally accountable and responsible for the learning of each student, and must do whatever it takes to get their job done. Mentees need help understanding that the work of teaching extends far beyond the school day. Initiative, dependability, and accountability are critical attributes that mentees need to pay attention to in order to get their job done.

SUMMARY

In this chapter, we have explored three different components of effective mentoring—creating a mentoring context, guiding professional knowledge development, and nurturing professional dispositions. The three components of effective mentoring are summarized in Figure 2.1. Through examining each component of effective mentoring, we learned that, like an onion, each of these components also has multiple layers. To create a mentoring context, mentors must provide mentees with emotional support, develop a strong relationship with their mentee, and ascertain a mentee's prior knowledge. To guide a mentee's professional knowledge development, mentors must pay attention to seven different types of knowledge—content, pedagogical, student learner, curriculum, pedagogical content, context, and classroom management. To nurture professional dispositions, mentees must cultivate a commitment to equity, inquiry, and collaboration, as well as a strong work ethic. Looking at all the layers that are a part of effective mentoring and that we have peeled apart in this chapter, like the cook peeling back the onion, you may be about to cry. Effective mentoring is so complex that it will become challenging!

Don't despair. Feeling challenged as you mentor is as natural as beginning teachers feeling challenged as they teach. Just like becoming an effective teacher, becoming an effective mentor is accomplished through careful thought and reflection about what you know and believe about mentoring, observing master mentor teachers at work, and reflecting once again on your own mentoring practice. We've created this book in response to the complexity mentoring entails—and to provide opportunities for you to reflect on mentoring and observe powerful mentors.

As you end this chapter, we once again provide exercises for you to reflect on your mentoring. The exercises afford you the opportunity to consider what you know about and believe about mentoring based on what you have read and what you have experienced as a mentor in the past.

Since mentoring is a private activity and it is difficult to ever observe someone in the act of mentoring, in Chapters 3 through 9, we provide you with glimpses of effective mentors in action. Honoring the logistical factors that complicate mentoring, these glimpses are from different school contexts and mentoring programs. The mentors

Figure 2.1 Three Components of Effective Mentoring

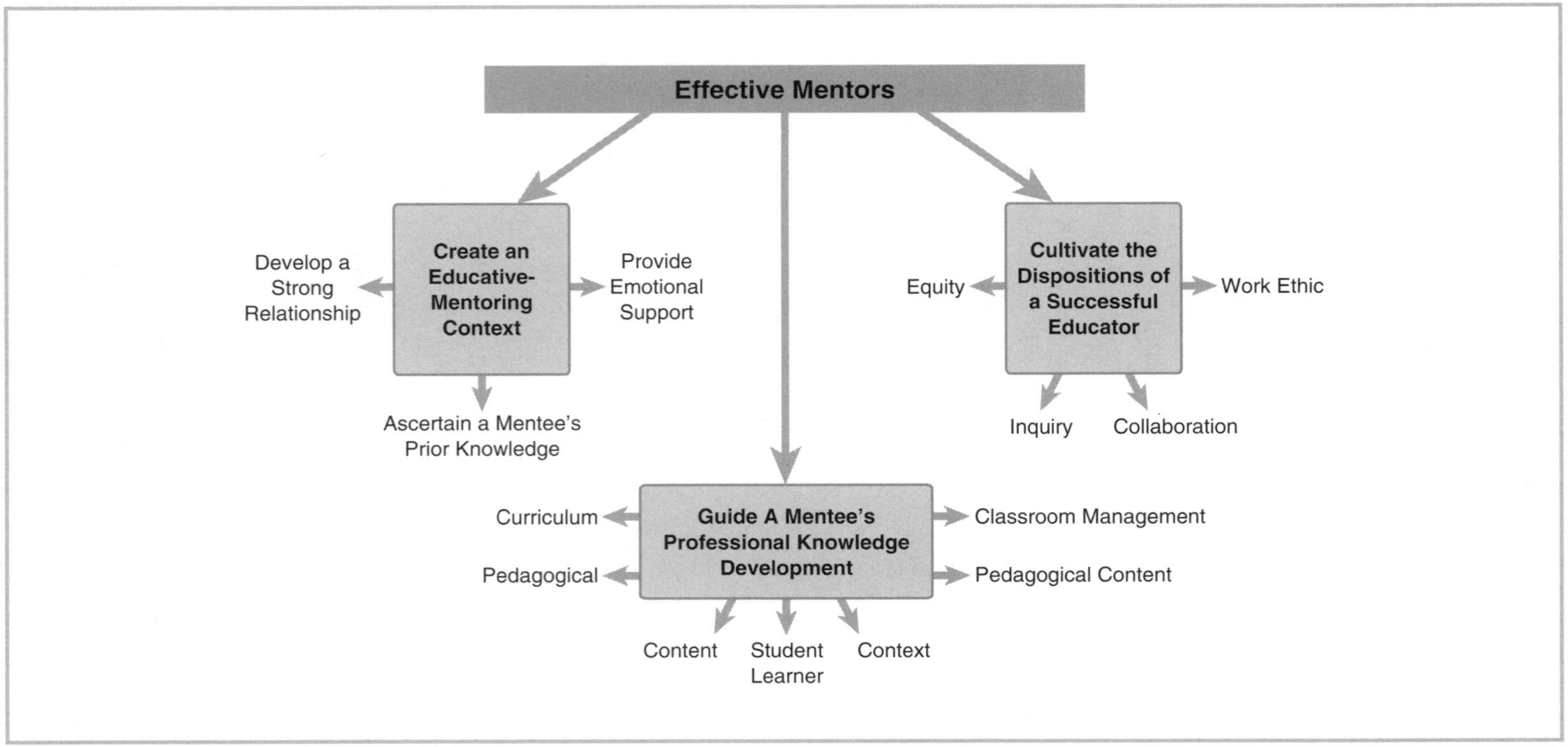

Effective Mentors

Create an Educative-Mentoring Context
- Develop a Strong Relationship
- Provide Emotional Support
- Ascertain a Mentee's Prior Knowledge

Cultivate the Dispositions of a Successful Educator
- Equity
- Work Ethic
- Inquiry
- Collaboration

Guide A Mentee's Professional Knowledge Development
- Curriculum
- Pedagogical
- Content
- Student Learner
- Context
- Classroom Management
- Pedagogical Content

are male and female, as well as elementary, middle, and high school teachers. The mentees they work with vary in life experiences and background. Each of the glimpses are either written by or based on a real-life mentor teacher.

Throughout these glimpses, you will see examples of the components of effective mentoring we've discussed in this chapter. In addition to these mentoring components, through each glimpse you will also view the art of mentoring through an exploration of different metaphors effective mentors use to conceptualize their mentoring practice. At the end of each chapter are questions for discussion that will help you explore the complexity of mentoring. Through discussion of these questions with others, you gain deeper insight into a particular mentor and his or her metaphor for mentoring as well as apply what you learn from each individual glimpse to the development of your own mentor identity.

There is an awful lot that goes into effective mentoring. Consider how educational researchers Jian Wang and Sandra Odell (2002) summarize the work of a mentor:

> First, mentors can engage novices in reflective interactions by focusing on specific events and teaching situations. Second, mentors can challenge novices to reexamine the crucial events and situations of teaching or learning to teach and can challenge them to reinterpret or reconstruct their meaning from the perspective of constructivist teaching. Third, mentors can offer alternative interpretations for events and situations and model the reflective process necessary for discovering the alternative interpretations and methods of decision making that are important in resolving teaching problems. Fourth, mentors can engage novices in such interactive reflections constantly and flexibly in a way that is consistent with where the novices are in learning to teach and where they need to go. (Wang & Odell, 2002, p. 524)

As you continue to develop the mentoring platform you created in Chapter 1, and use this platform to analyze and discuss the mentors that appear in this book, some of the complexity of mentoring is untangled, you strengthen your skills as a mentor, and you emerge as a more effective mentor teacher. Your more complete mentoring will build a more effective future teaching workforce. A more effective future teaching workforce will lead to a more effective education for *all* children!

Chapter 2 Exercises

1. Think back to your own experiences as a mentor. What are your most vivid memories? How do they connect or disconnect to the components of effective mentoring described in this chapter?

2. Think back to your own experiences being mentored. What are your most vivid memories? How do they connect or disconnect to the components of effective mentoring described in this chapter?

3. How does the mentoring platform that you developed in the Chapter 1 exercises compare to and contrast with the components of effective mentoring described in this chapter?

3

Mentor as Story-Weaver

The Case of Darby

With Darby Claire Delane

THE MENTOR

Darby is a White middle school teacher who has taught adolescents for nearly ten years. Her experience as a teacher in "at risk," special, and general education classrooms has led her to push strongly for inclusive practices in her school. She currently teaches eighth-grade U.S. history as a general educator, and is known for her ability to differentiate curriculum in order to accommodate a wide spectrum of learners. Darby's classroom is often the first entry point for students with physical, emotional, and learning special needs who have had little success in the world of general education. In addition, she serves many gifted students as well as wide ranges of linguistically, culturally, and socioeconomically diverse adolescents.

Darby believes teaching is inherently a political act, and she takes this charge seriously. She is strongly committed to social justice in the public schools, and insists that her classes remain as diverse as possible. She says her classroom is a place where "we *do* democracy," which she sees as a rigorous and daily goal. Darby and her students work to find and develop "voice," provide respect and space for all emerging voices, engage in collaborative learning experiences, and allow for a regular fare of multiple perspectives. She blends her history curriculum with strong, varied literacy practices so that learning is accessible to and meaningful for all students.

THE MENTEE

Esteban, a Cuban American from Miami, Florida, was the most unique student teacher Darby had ever hosted in her eighth-grade history classroom. He was 23 years old, and was looking forward to becoming a secondary school social studies teacher in the public schools, even though he had attended a private, all-boys Jesuit school. Esteban's Hispanic identity, his love for hip-hop music, and his commitment to sports made him instantly fascinating to Darby's adolescent students. Esteban saw himself as a potential school leader, and he planned to return to the Miami community to teach high school, coach basketball, and eventually enter administration, as his father had done.

From the start of his internship, Esteban expressed concerns to Darby about his ability to become a teacher. He told her he had a short temper and, in the not-so-distant past, he had had problems with fighting in Miami, a skill he valued as necessary in the social world in which he grew up. Now these values were in direct conflict with the ways in which he was being socialized as a public school teacher. He didn't know where to "put" this part of himself, and had nowhere he could express these concerns during his program. In addition, he deeply defended the strict discipline methods that were displayed by his Jesuit priest teachers in secondary school. These included public humiliation, corporal punishment, and teacher use of explicit language. He felt at a loss when it came to learning new management strategies and hoped Darby could help him expand his repertoire.

Darby knew Esteban would present new challenges for her as a cooperating teacher. However, what excited Darby about her new student teacher was that he appeared reflective, sensitive, and open to frank conversations. She decided that the most salient issue was that Esteban needed to become conscious of, then critically evaluate, his incoming belief system of what power and authority looks like for a teacher. Her job would be to help Esteban begin to construct his identity as a professional teacher in a public school system he did not yet understand. She realized that she would have to literally become a cultural broker for Esteban, and that she would need to work quickly to begin his socialization process. This would be tricky. How was she going to help Esteban transform his belief system without suggesting his incoming beliefs were somehow inferior or bad? In addition, so much of Esteban's unique personality and cultural capital would be an asset to his emerging professional identity. How would she help him negotiate some of these unique assets into his new identity?

THE CONTEXT

Esteban was placed in Darby's eighth-grade classroom in a suburban middle school as a student teacher. He was experiencing the end of his five-year master's program at the local university. Darby receives tuition vouchers as compensation from the university for her work with Esteban. Esteban was a member of a close cohort of students who had been going through their secondary social studies program together. Darby was also a graduate student at the university, and had the pleasure of taking a course with Esteban and his cohort the semester before he started interning in her classroom. This offered Darby a unique preview of Esteban and how he "fit" with other preservice teachers in his peer group. It also gave her a glimpse of the kinds of methods he was being taught and expected to use, which she would later reinforce in the classroom with him. Being a member of both of Esteban's worlds—the academic world of his university program and the "real-life" world of her classroom—was valuable in their work together, offering a depth to their dialogue that may not have happened otherwise.

Esteban was expected to teach nearly all day in Darby's U.S. history classes for ten weeks. In order to support their mentoring experience, Darby introduced what she called a "reflective journal," which they would use to write back and forth to one another, ensuring a minimum daily dialogue. Darby's students also contributed to Esteban's development by providing written and spoken reflections on his pedagogical methods and teaching style, as well as their ideas on the whole business of teaching and learning. In addition, a "lunchtime dialogue group" began to form as three other adults began joining Esteban and Darby during lunch for naturally occurring, lively dialogue sessions about daily experiences and teaching ideas. These adults included Darby's own mentor teacher, a first-year teacher from next door, and another intern from a different social studies classroom. Finally, Esteban was introduced early to Darby's video camera, which they called the "teacher cam." The teacher cam evolved into a powerful and enjoyable tool, used informally to create an almost–reality TV experience that they nicknamed "Esteban: Teacher-in-the-Making." Darby, Esteban, and their students operated the camera and viewed taped segments throughout the internship. Shots incorporated classroom scenes and interviews involving students, Esteban, Darby, and other members of the learning community. The journal, student participation, lunchtime dialogue group, and teacher cam significantly heightened the level of metacognition among all participants, creating a space for a partnership of learning that Darby had never experienced before within her classroom.

One of the first things that Darby came to discover while filming Esteban was his love for telling stories. Esteban made history lessons come alive for the students with his stories, often acting them by using the entire space of the room. He incorporated body language, linguistic variations, students as characters, and everyday classroom objects that happened to be there. Darby soon recognized his storytelling gift as a powerful asset for the emerging teacher he was becoming. She also believed that getting Esteban to tell stories about his own Catholic school experiences would help draw out the valuable raw material needed to understand his unique, incoming belief system about discipline.

During planning periods, Darby encouraged Esteban to "perform" on the teacher cam his stories of his Catholic school. Esteban acted them out with the same drama and humor he used with the students, bringing his Jesuit priest "characters" to life. She wanted to draw out these stories from Esteban carefully, without judgment, so that they could begin looking at them from a public school perspective. Often, Esteban's stories would be the entertaining topic of the lunchtime dialogue group, since three out of the five members had also experienced Catholic school while growing up. The weaving nature of the telling of and listening to these stories was grounded in a common need to negotiate these early school experiences with the expectations they now had as public school teachers. The co-construction of "what it means to be a teacher in public school" that occurred during these lunches scaffolded Esteban's development in a way that Darby could never have done alone.

THE METAPHOR: A STORY-WEAVER

The work of the storyteller is typically described using a weaving metaphor. Esteban was definitely a storyteller in the sense that he could "tell yarns" and "spin tales." Darby wanted to use Esteban's stories to help him evaluate his incoming belief system, and to ultimately co-construct his professional identity with the support and contributions of their colleagues and students. However, Darby knew that simply letting him tell stories was not going to make this happen within a short, ten-week period. She was going to have to figure out how she could take an active role in accelerating the potential for those stories to become vehicles for Esteban's transformation into a professional educator.

Darby began to conceptualize her mentoring task with Esteban as paralleling the work of a weaver. Darby knew that all weavers must accomplish two basic goals when producing fabric. First, they must do the careful work of "spinning," which means to draw out and twist fibers into a continuous yarn or thread. In the hearing or reading of stories, we often look for "the running thread," or theme. Darby worked to identify and then spin the common themes from within Esteban's stories. She could not attend to all of the themes his stories expressed, but she could pull out the ones that were the most salient. Esteban's most common themes invariably involved feelings of powerlessness or helplessness surrounding his need for establishing his authority with students.

Second, weavers take their threads and weave them together to form a fabric that holds a particular pattern, texture, and size. The "cloth" Darby wanted to help Esteban weave would represent his developing professional identity as a public school educator. She knew Esteban was going to need help in weaving this cloth. He would need the contributions of many other threads to give it the strength and form necessary to carry him to his first job. Darby struggled with how to introduce different perspectives and spin them into usable threads in a way that would not threaten to overpower or eliminate Esteban's own uniqueness.

Using the storytelling forum, she invited others to tell their own stories. Darby worked to explicitly spin out common themes by drawing Esteban's attention to them, then weaving them together with their reflective work. Esteban heard stories about classroom management experiences from both students and the lunchtime dialogue group. Darby also told her own stories to him. She reinforced these tales by daily, consistent modeling of her own belief system concerning classroom management. This belief system did not need to incorporate the shaming or making students feel "lesser," because she did not believe that these kind of teacher behaviors demonstrated control. She placed a great deal of trust in the ability of adolescents to make good choices with their behavior, and wanted Esteban to understand how empowering this belief was for both her students and for her.

Darby's greatest effort went into helping Esteban actively weave the multiple threads offered by the different perspectives into a single fabric of meaning that would suit Esteban's needs. Through their commitment to daily reflection, they worked to tease out ("spin") themes that Esteban wanted to incorporate into his own perspective. It was at this point that Esteban would show his ability to *re*story, or *re*script his own ideas about what it meant to be a teacher and hold authority, and what that would look like in his behaviors and words. She knew that the "weaving" of these themes, or "threads," was successfully in progress when she could see evidence of Esteban's rescripting. This evidence would show up in the way he would reduce his judgmental tendencies when interpreting student behaviors, as well as the positive changes he made in his own behavior when interacting with students.

A GLIMPSE OF DARBY, ESTEBAN, AND THE STORY-WEAVER METAPHOR IN ACTION

As mentioned earlier, one of Esteban's main recurring themes was his struggle with what he labeled as "disrespect" from some students, and how he felt powerless to assert what he believed to be "effective discipline" within the constraints of public school. Esteban did not see public school management options as strict enough, and he feared he would never be able to establish himself as an authority figure without the more aggressive tactics his Jesuit teachers had been able to use. Interestingly, one of the most difficult students Esteban encountered during his internship was Jamal, a student he did not even teach or know.

One day, after a class Esteban taught that Darby had observed as having gone particularly well, Esteban seemed distraught. Darby was surprised that he had felt this way inside, and could not guess as to what had happened during class to make him feel so angry. He explained that what made him upset had occurred before class. He had had a run-in with an unknown student out in the hallway. As soon as he described the student, Darby knew Esteban had encountered Jamal. All teachers, sooner or later, "encountered" Jamal. Darby asked him if she could get the teacher cam so she could "get the story." He agreed, and Darby and Esteban began documenting the next story of "Esteban: Teacher-in-the-Making." A condensed version of the dialogue follows.

D: Tell me the story of Jamal in the hallway.

E: Is Jamal his name? My God, he pissed me off. He and a couple of his friends totally ignored me when I asked them to get to class. I said, "Guys, get to class." Then I said it again, louder: "GUYS, GET TO CLASS." Then Jamal said, "You can't f— make me." And, Darby, I just want to tell him off, you know? All this (adrenaline) comes up and I don't know what to do. I swear I just wanted to—God, I don't know. He doesn't **know** me—how can he think he can **talk** to me like that? He needs to be suspended or expelled or something.

D: Tell me the rest of the story.

E: That's it.

D: No it's not. What happened next?

E: Nothing happened next. They walked away and I had to come in and start teaching class.

D: Exactly—you came in and started teaching class. That's right. And you didn't lose your temper. You didn't curse at him. You came in and started teaching. And I had no idea you were so angry. Neither did the kids. We never even knew. What's up with that?

(Continued)

(Continued)

> E: *Well, I had to teach class. I didn't think it was something I should bring into the classroom.*
>
> D: *That sounds like a teacher to me—a professional. How did you do that?*
>
> E: *I gotta' do my job, you know? I can't let that sh— get in the way of my kids.*
>
> At this point, Darby cast a new thread into the weaving of Esteban's story about Jamal:
>
> D: *Okay, so my intern is telling me the story about a kid in the hallway. He's trying to get kids to class, and this boy won't go to class and, in fact, becomes defiant. Esteban knows this is not cool for a student to get away with talking to an adult this way, and knows the kid must be held accountable for his behaviors. This kid's name is Jamal, but he doesn't know that yet. Jamal has almost been kicked out of the school many times for aggressive, even violent, behavior. He's super smart, but his emotional issues keep him in all ESE classes. His mom and dad aren't there because they abandoned Jamal and his sisters when he was two. After they left, he had to live in a bunch of foster homes, where he was physically and sexually abused over and over. Now he lives with his sister, who we're pretty sure has to work as a prostitute to make ends meet. I heard him tell his ESE teacher that the biggest goal he has ever had in his life was to be able to walk across the stage and graduate from eighth grade.*
>
> E: *My God, Darby, I didn't know all that.*
>
> D: *Yeah, most teachers don't know all that about Jamal. You want to know more about him?*
>
> E: *Yeah, tell me.*
>
> D: *Well, I can't, because I don't know much more than that. You will have to go meet him and find out for yourself. I would like you to come back and tell me the rest of the story.*

Later that day, the lunchtime dialogue group dropped by. Darby asked Esteban to again tell the story of Jamal. However, Darby put a new spin on the next thread to be introduced. This time, she intentionally framed her request from the position of a proud cooperating teacher, a stance that genuinely expressed how she felt. She began with the words, "You would not believe how well Esteban handled this situation today." Then she said, "Esteban, tell them the story of Jamal in the hallway."

She was actively spinning a new theme, or thread, by inviting Esteban to rescript his original story, steeped in a sense of power-lessness, to a newer version where he was encouraged to recognize how power*ful* he had actually acted. She was giving him a space to focus on the fact that he had not been "beaten" by Jamal, but had, instead, been able to maintain his composure and attend to his pri-mary responsibility: that of walking into the classroom and *teaching his students, no matter what.* Esteban's retelling of the story was important to Darby, because she wanted him to hear his own voice describing how he had been able to maintain professionalism, no matter how disrupted he felt inside. In addition, she wanted to see him restory in front of an audience he trusted and valued the opin-ions of. In this way, he would hopefully feel more accountable for acting on his emerging scripts of the "responsible, professional teacher," since there would be a group waiting to hear how similar stories would unfold.

There was no doubt that Esteban still needed to find a resolu-tion with Jamal. He was right. Jamal *should* have to answer for his behavior. The next day, Darby located Jamal and asked him if he would be willing to talk about what happened with Esteban. Darby was surprised when Jamal agreed. She had no idea how the ending of this story would develop, but she had to trust that the two of them could figure it out for themselves. It was time to move out of the way and let Esteban test the newly woven "cloth" of his pro-fessional identity.

After Esteban and Jamal talked, Esteban went on the teacher cam to tell the next part of the story. With his typical ability to bring the context of his stories alive, Esteban spoke to the camera and described how he and Jamal had had a talk "man-to-man." Esteban had located Jamal at lunch, sat down, and ate with him. He asked Jamal what had happened the day before. Jamal talked about *his* story. Right before Esteban had met up with him in the hallway, he had just gotten in trouble with his teacher, who had found a very private note from his girlfriend. Jamal said he didn't appreciate being "yelled at" by Esteban at that particular moment, because he thought he was about to get suspended—*again.* Esteban was then able to relate to Jamal how angry he felt when Jamal didn't listen to him, and that he thought it was his job to make sure all students got to class on time, no matter what. He said what bothered him the most was that Jamal had spoken to him with such blatant disrespect, and he didn't even know Esteban. They continued their talk about how school was hard for Jamal, and how difficult it was to stay out of trouble. Esteban shared that he, too, had gotten into trouble a lot in school. Esteban spoke about some of the things he had come to understand that had helped him later to improve his life. At the end of their talk, Esteban said that Jamal offered a genuine apology for cursing at him in the hallway. Esteban was stunned. He told the camera, "I never saw *that* one coming."

A week later, Darby asked Esteban, once again, to "tell the story of Jamal" to the lunchtime group. This time, the story did not even include the incident in the hallway. Instead, Esteban's "story about Jamal" talked about how he was coming in to see Esteban every day before school to talk about basketball scores. The members of the lunchtime group could not believe that Jamal would choose to talk to Esteban, or any teacher, for that matter. The character of Esteban's story, "Jamal," had been recast as the story evolved, changing from a disrespectful "punk" to a student trying desperately to survive and find a reason to trust *any* adult in his life.

Esteban was following a new thread deep into the complex social concept of respect. He was coming to see that not all kids believed adults were worthy of respect, simply based on their position as adults. Perhaps respect was something that had to be built over time. Perhaps it was not an automatic given, and needed to be earned by *all* parties involved. And while students must be held accountable for their actions, perhaps adults could reflect on their part in how the actions of students played out. Maybe within this deeper investigation of respect, and how it is cocreated, was where a more stable source of power, authority, and positive influence lay for Esteban.

Darby as story-weaver was helping Esteban co-construct the possibility of a powerful new belief system that valued a more democratic, collaborative space for the nurturing of student respect than he had learned from his authoritarian Jesuit school. Esteban's willingness to widen his perceptions of Jamal had shown strong evidence of hard work in rescripting his old views about gaining respect. Esteban was able to draw from a much wider base of interpretation through the various threads Darby introduced, allowing him to have a larger repertoire of possible responses.

Esteban was literally transforming into a powerful teacher, mentor, and life coach. Jamal was not even a student Esteban was required to be responsible for, yet he *became* responsible for Jamal with that first hallway interaction. What Esteban did with that responsibility was critical. Darby hoped Esteban would take his amazing story with him and tell it over and over, collecting more stories that reinforced his newfound power as a teacher and change agent.

Darby the story-weaver was transformed as well, into an even more responsive mentor and teacher. Esteban taught Darby to respect the power of the incoming belief systems of her interns, reminding her that preservice teachers never show up with blank pages to be written on. He helped her to see the kind of mentoring that can come from active listening, convincing her to always carve out enough time for preservice teachers to share their stories. She saw the power within storytelling to reveal the scripts that are embedded within them, and the salient themes that they would give rise to. Esteban's presence and differing values also provoked a depth of dialogue with her colleagues and students that she would never forget. The challenges Esteban brought to Darby as a mentor reaffirmed her faith in how responsible, caring reflection and dialogue can act as one of the most powerful vehicles for learning and transformation available to human beings.

SUMMARY

Mentoring is a complex endeavor. Every mentor and mentee is different. Consequently, every mentor-mentee relationship is different. If a mentor is a story-weaver, that mentor will . . .

1. elicit the personal stories mentees bring with them that shape their beliefs about teaching.

2. help mentees "story" critical incidents that occur as they learn to teach through such venues as reflective journaling, storytelling to peers, and being videotaped.

3. help mentees frame and reframe their stories to come to deeper and richer understandings of what their stories mean in relationship to their beliefs and in relationship to their development as a teacher.

For Discussion

1. One critical component of mentoring using a story-weaver metaphor is its power to elicit the initial story with which a mentee enters teaching—your mentee's past experiences as well as the beliefs about teaching and learning your mentee has developed as a result of these experiences.

- What are some ways you could elicit your mentee's initial story?

- What are some common beliefs about teaching and learning that mentees often enter the teaching professions with that could benefit from being reshaped, reframed, and restoried?

2. Once Esteban's initial story is told, Darby incorporates some creative mentoring pedagogy to provide opportunities for Esteban to restory, including journaling, the teacher cam, and lunchtime dialogue groups.

- What are the benefits and drawbacks of each one of these mentor pedagogical strategies?

- How and when might you use these three mentoring strategies in your current mentoring context?

- What are some other strategies you might use to help a mentee learn and grow as a teacher through restorying?

3. What elements of the mentee/mentor relationship would be essential to facilitate mentee growth using the story-weaver metaphor?

4. What components of effective mentoring (creating an educative mentoring context, guiding a mentee's professional knowledge development, and nurturing the development of a mentee's professional dispositions) are evident in this metaphor?

5. List the strengths and limitations of conceptualizing mentoring using a story-weaver metaphor.

6. Regardless of your own mentoring context, what can you learn from this story to inform your own mentoring practice?

4

Mentor as Jigsaw Puzzle Enthusiast

The Case of Kevin

With Kevin Berry

THE MENTOR

Kevin is a male teacher in his eighth year of teaching. He has taught at the same rural elementary school with many children whose first language is not English and whose families follow Hari Krishna teaching. Kevin taught third grade for one year, and has since taught fourth grade. Before becoming a full-time teacher, Kevin substitute taught in middle school, and was briefly an aide in a special education classroom. Kevin finds himself regularly questioning his own teaching as he focuses on improvement, and he is currently pursuing an advanced degree at the University, and is teaching a methods course to prospective teachers. He constantly concerns himself with whether or not the beliefs in his teaching platform are reflected in his practice. Kevin aspires to create an inclusive, democratic classroom community. He hopes to address the needs of all of his students, balancing external pedagogical requirements (i.e., state and local mandates) with his own methods of constructivist teaching. As Kevin has hosted all levels of field experiences in his classroom, mentoring traditional student teachers, practicum students, and full-year interns, he has made his struggle to balance these factors and make his thinking visible to his mentees. This year, Kevin was selected by his principal to provide support for four new teachers in his building.

THE MENTEES

Tina is an enthusiastic, motivated, 22-year-old first-grade teacher who just graduated from a teacher education program. Her ultimate goal is to help bridge the gap in educational attainment between those students from lower and higher socioeconomic households. She tutors children after school and is very busy.

Joseph is a 24-year-old fourth-grade teacher and former soccer player. He changed his major while he was in college a few times before deciding that his heart is with helping children and entering a teacher education program. Now, in this first teaching position, he is very confident in whatever he does.

Margaret is a 31-year-old fourth-grade teacher. She has previous military experience and entered this first job through the Troops to Teaching Program, and is now very motivated to become the teacher she has always wanted to become. She is dedicated to helping children learn, but has had limited experience collaborating with other teachers.

Crystal is a 45-year-old third-grade teacher. She is a part of a one-year, district-directed alternative certification program, has raised her daughter, and is now ready to begin her career. She drives nearly two hours to school every day, but is completely dedicated to the students in her classroom. Her biggest concern is that she is going to "mess up" and harm the students academically.

THE CONTEXT

Kevin enjoys mentoring new teachers in his rural elementary school and engages in mentoring on a regular basis. Each of these novices arrive at his school with very distinct background experiences and pathways to the teaching profession. These new inductees are experiencing their first year as classroom teachers in Kevin's building, and he has been assigned to work with them as a part of the new teacher induction program in his district. As part of the new teacher induction program, seasoned veteran teachers receive extra compensation to work with first-year teachers. Kevin meets once a month with these new teachers as a group to provide information about district paperwork, policy, and procedures. Kevin is also provided with a substitute teacher one to two days a month so that he is freed up from his classroom responsibilities to observe his mentees in action. In addition, Kevin sometimes uses his "specials" time to observe these new teachers. Finally, Kevin meets individually with each teacher after school as often as he can, but at least once a month, to check in more informally, listen to his mentee's experiences, help troubleshoot problems, and provide support. Given extra compensation and a substitute teacher once a month, the district frames his responsibilities as helping the new teachers in his building be both successful with children and survive the system of public schools.

THE METAPHOR: A JIGSAW PUZZLE ENTHUSIAST

Since a mentoring relationship is so complex, one may liken it to a jigsaw puzzle. Many intricate pieces must come together to attain a cohesive, collaborative learning relationship. In order for a mentor to take the most active role in this relationship, a mentor might need to assume the role of a jigsaw puzzle enthusiast. This person is not someone who just sits around for hours eventually slopping together the pieces, but rather is one who meticulously and deliberately places each piece in just the right place. He cannot and will not rest until all the pieces are safely where they belong and the masterpiece is complete.

This action requires logical thinking along with a caring, thoughtful touch. A mentor must first figure out what kind of teacher and person the mentee is. Then he must find out what kind of teacher and person that mentee wants to become. Puzzle pieces, like relationships and trust, are often delicate and easily broken. A jigsaw puzzle enthusiast never forces pieces together. In this mentor-mentee relationship, the mentor helps the mentee decide for himself exactly what kind of growth should take place. The mentor will then guide the mentee in what he perceives to be the right direction. Before attempting to connect the pieces, the enthusiast should take care that the pieces are compatible. In this relationship, the mentor is sure that the actions fit the teacher's platforms, adhere to research-based practices, and suit the current teaching context. Perhaps the most difficult part about being a mentor is discovering exactly which pieces are present and what you want the puzzle to look like when you are finished.

A GLIMPSE OF KEVIN, TINA, AND THE JIGSAW PUZZLE ENTHUSIAST METAPHOR IN ACTION

Tina was a true go-getter. Some might have even called her a natural. She loved students, loved teaching, and would do everything she could to make sure her students enjoyed learning. Kevin's and her mentor-mentee relationship was as tight as they come. They taught right next door to each other and shared a small office space. They had mutual respect for one another; they depended on each other; they trusted each other. Still, a piece of the puzzle was missing. Tina always seemed to take personally any unforeseen or undesired event that happened during a lesson.

After Kevin completed an observation of Tina one day, she started sobbing. Kevin thought the lesson about fractions had been very successful. All the students seemed to grasp the objectives very well. He was shocked by Tina's discontent.

"Did you see what Nick did? I spent hours trying to make sure he wouldn't do it. But he did it anyway. I tried so hard to make sure that he wouldn't throw the clay, but he did anyway."

To be honest, Kevin had not even noticed that Nick had thrown the clay.

K: What did you do about it when it happened?

T: It was as we were cleaning up. I gave him a "Number 3" and told him that we would have to talk about it at recess. Then I asked him to pick up the clay he threw and put it in the trash can. I also told him that he would have to miss part of the activity the next time we used clay. He would use something else instead.

K: Those seem like appropriate, even natural, consequences. So what's the problem?

T: The problem is that I want to prevent things like that from happening. I know that's the best way to manage students' behavior. I also don't want to see him get in trouble all the time like he does when he goes to specials. I failed.

Tina had definitely assumed responsibility for the actions of her students. However, at some point Kevin thought she needed to realize that she cannot solve all the problems all the time. In fact, he was afraid that if she always attributed every minor defeat to her own actions, without noticing all the positive aspects of what came from what she did, she probably would spend many of her afternoons crying. Until this moment, Kevin never knew that she actually expected to prevent every kind of student misbehavior or misconception.

K: Do you think you can always have everything go exactly the way you planned it?

T: No, but I feel as though I should be able to do it most of the time if I'm a good teacher. I especially want to help kids like Nick.

K: That's understandable . . . but what about the other 24 who learned about numerators and denominators?

T: I guess.

K: Tina, let me tell you something I have learned about teaching. Perfection is great, but it's not reality. There will always be something that happens that you didn't want to happen. There will always be a teachable moment you think about afterward that you might have missed. There will always be an accommodation you forgot to make. That's been my experience, anyway.

T: But I feel as if I should be able to help everyone learn—everyone know how to be a good citizen, all the time.

K: *That's what makes you such a good teacher. Think of all the good you've done. Think of all that your students have learned.*

T: *I guess.*

K: *Tina, you know I have this saying about the success of lessons. Some lessons are more successful than others, but the only unsuccessful lessons are the ones in which you cannot find anything to change the next time. What else can you try to help prevent Nick from throwing clay in the next activity?*

As a result of his dialogue with Tina and observations of Tina's teaching during the course of the year, Kevin knew that Tina was on her way to being an excellent, experienced teacher. He knew she researched content knowledge before teaching. He knew she used a variety of teaching methods, including technology. He knew she expressed clear learning goals for her students, and he knew she made many accommodations for student learning. What he did not know, however, could have been the one piece of the puzzle that caused Tina to leave the teaching profession early. If she actually thought she failed every time anything went wrong, Kevin did not believe she would be able to emotionally survive in teaching for very long at all.

From then on, Kevin was able to lead co-reflection discussions focusing on all the student learning and positive behavior outcomes. Afterward, he then steered the conversation toward change for next time. Without this piece of the puzzle, Kevin might not have been able to help his mentee meet her learning needs. She needed to know that she is responsible for the learning of her students, but in reality, nothing is perfect all the time—no matter how talented the teacher.

The true problem here was finding the missing piece of the puzzle. Somewhere, buried in the pile, was just the right piece to complete the masterpiece. Sometimes the hardest pieces to find are the ones that you may not even realize are missing.

A GLIMPSE OF KEVIN, JOSEPH, AND THE JIGSAW PUZZLE ENTHUSIAST METAPHOR IN ACTION

Joseph was cool, calm, and composed. No matter what confronted him, he stood relaxed and undaunted. At times, some might think he should feel a little nervous, a little concerned, a little unprepared. He never did. Joseph looked at teaching as an obligation that needed to be accomplished. He arrived, worked on the task, and when he thought he was finished (when his time in front of the kids was over), he could do what he wanted to do. In other words, work was something you had to do, but once you finished it, you were able to play. Kevin thought this was just the way Joseph was at this stage in his life, and he thought Joseph might change his philosophy as he matured as a teacher. At the beginning of the year, Kevin noticed that Joseph would arrive when the "work" began, and would leave as soon as he felt that he was done. For example, the last bell did not ring until 7:45 a.m., and even though he was to be there at 7:15, he often strolled in around 7:25. Joseph did not feel that he should be there until there was actually work to do with students. Planning time began at 10:40, and Joseph typically spent that time on the phone arranging the adult soccer league schedule that he ran part-time after school. Finally, even though the teaching contract said that he should stay until 3:15 p.m., if there were no students in the classroom, he often would go home early. The time on the clock had no meaning for him, since putting in time when students were not present was not his idea of what teaching was about. While Kevin did not necessarily share Joseph's philosophy about life and teaching, he respected Joseph's right to see things from a different perspective, until it became evident that Joseph's lack of time put into teaching outside of the time he spent with children was affecting his instruction and his relationship with other faculty. If Kevin had never discovered that Joseph framed his new profession like a "job," he probably would have been completely unable to relate to him. However, after identifying this puzzle piece, Kevin had to take some direct action.

After an observation of a mediocre lesson taught directly from following the teacher plan book, and receiving some comments from colleagues about his mentee's apparent lack of effort, Kevin arranged for mentor-mentee meetings and tasks to be completed before school. Kevin was surprised when Joseph's punctuality changed. If Joseph had something he felt was important enough to do, he would see to it that he was there. Kevin changed the way he worked with Joseph in order to help Joseph see the difference planning can make to his teaching and student learning. Kevin wrote down an explicit and prioritized list of the tasks he always accomplished during planning times, before, during, and after school. The next day, he sat down with Joseph and talked through the list. He gave a copy of the list to Joseph, and together they made a daily checklist of what Joseph would complete. Some tasks just had to be done before the bell rang, and others had to be completed when the students were at specials, while still others happened after students left for the day. As a result, Joseph arrived on time more often and usually stayed until the end of the teacher workday.

Since Joseph also looked at teaching in terms of the work done in the classroom with the students, he did not understand that preparation time or planning was part of teaching. Because he had never witnessed the thoroughness of the teacher planning process, he did not recognize the amount of effort and energy that needed to go into planning. After discovering this, Kevin began asking Joseph to meet Fridays after school to share his lesson plans for the next week. At that point, they began to share ideas, and that collaborative dialogue about their weekly plans deepened Joseph's understanding of his planning responsibilities. As a result, Kevin reshaped Joseph's focus on planning and eventually accrued ample evidence of preparation and planning.

If Kevin had never found these pieces of the puzzle, he probably would have tossed all the pieces around the room in frustration. However, even though the scene of this completed puzzle might not be as pretty as others, it did get finished. Students learned, and the mentor and mentee grew professionally.

A GLIMPSE OF KEVIN, MARGARET, AND THE JIGSAW PUZZLE ENTHUSIAST METAPHOR IN ACTION

Margaret had great potential. She was bright and capable. She really wanted to do her best to help her students learn. Working with others, however, was something she did not feel comfortable doing. She explained that her military training emphasized that she assume responsibility for what was going on, and the only way she could manage to do her best was to be in complete control of every situation.

Because Margaret always wanted to be in control, she rarely sought to collaborate with others, including her mentor, Kevin. When he attempted to coplan with her, she cheerfully said she would take care of it by herself. In fact, Kevin felt as if he was intruding whenever he offered any unsolicited ideas or suggestions. Kevin felt that this collaborative avoidance was a huge problem. Aside from the fact that he thought that the only way to be a good teacher was to share ideas about student learning with other teachers, Kevin was further concerned because Margaret taught in an inclusive classroom. Her control issues prevented her from collaborating with the exceptional student education teachers. Without the expertise of the ESE specialists, Margaret would miss out on learning new strategies her students with disabilities needed. She would be unable to benefit from other teachers' countless years of expertise and insight.

Kevin did not know how he could get this piece of the puzzle to fit with the others. He tried a variety of plans to get Margaret to understand that she could only truly be in control when she gave up a little control and shared the responsibility with others. Without collaboration, she would never be able to meet the diverse needs of her students. Kevin tried modeling how he coplanned with others. He tried creating action plans to help facilitate coplanning between Margaret and other teachers. Still, she felt as though she was better able to work alone.

Finally, the moment arrived. One morning, Margaret appeared especially worried. Kevin approached her to find out what was wrong.

M: I'm looking at these test scores. I don't know why Gordon and Matt aren't doing better. They must not be trying.

K: That's possible. What have you tried to do to motivate them?

M: They miss recess whenever they don't finish their work. I've called their parents. I've done all sorts of things. I can't do anything else. I'm out of ideas.

K: Well, maybe you could talk to the teachers they had last year. Perhaps they have an idea about what works for them.

M: I don't know. I guess I could. I'll go home and think about it. Maybe I'll come up with something else. I know I can think of something.

K: Not everyone has all the ideas, Margaret. Sometimes it's much more efficient to have others do a little problem solving with you. Last year's teacher may know the trick. I'm sure she can offer some advice.

M: Maybe.

Margaret went home and came up with a new idea. She awarded the students a sticker for every ten minutes they were on task. After ten stickers, the students got a jolly rancher. That seemed to help their behavior, but it didn't help their academic progress. After a couple of days, Margaret noticed the two students were still struggling on their reading assessments. At the same time, Margaret was experiencing a new issue with a few more students, and her stress showed in everything she did.

Kevin secretly arranged for Gordon and Matt's teacher from last year to stop by during lunch to ask how the students were doing. Margaret then explained all of her concerns to Mrs. Martin. She found out that Mrs. Martin had experienced similar dilemmas with the students last year. Mrs. Martin suggested that Margaret keep the students after school one day per week to give them extra help in the areas in which they were struggling.

Since Margaret's schedule did not allow her to work with them after school, she began to work with Gordon and Matt before school two mornings per week. One day Margaret chose the students' activities, and on the second day the students had the choice. After three weeks, she began to see a little improvement in their progress on the reading assessments. Margaret was most impressed, though, by Gordon and Matt's marked improvement in behavior. Kevin was most impressed by Margaret's willingness to follow through with a suggestion made by another teacher. Even though he had to secretly make arrangements to encourage that collaboration, he finally managed to finish the puzzle. Margaret found the missing piece.

A GLIMPSE OF KEVIN, CRYSTAL, AND THE JIGSAW PUZZLE ENTHUSIAST METAPHOR IN ACTION

Crystal loved her students. She wanted to do everything she could for them. Her utmost concern was having a good rapport with every single student. That relationship, however, was her only measure of success. No matter what, she was afraid of being "mean," and she was tortured if ever she thought a student was upset with her. Considering the realities of the classroom, this often left Crystal agonizing about how she could manage the students' behavior while ensuring none of them were ever mad at her.

This perspective was evident in almost every reflection discussion she and Kevin had with each other.

K: How do you think your lesson went?

C: I think the kids had fun. Everyone was smiling and laughing.

K: Motivating students is important. What evidence do you have for student learning?

C: Well, I listened to them as they were working in their groups, and they all seemed to understand.

K: That's good. What will you do to assess their learning?

C: I observed them.

K: Observation is good, but have you thought about other ways to assess the students beyond observation? There are multiple ways of assessing student learning. Just as we differentiate the way we teach, we can differentiate the way we assess them.

C: That makes sense. I think that Shelley is mad at me.

K: Mad at you? Why?

C: She was talking while I was giving directions, and I said something to her. I think she thought I was too mean.

K: Well, should she have been talking when you were giving directions?

C: No, but I'm sure it was an accident. I'll apologize to her.

K: Apologize to her? For what?

C: For getting onto her.

Although Kevin's own concern was Crystal's lack of attention to assessing student learning and inability to see the need for this as she plans for future instruction, Kevin realized there was a more immediate issue that needed to be resolved. In his observations of Crystal, Kevin had noticed that Crystal was often unwilling to correct student behavior if she thought the student would get upset with her. Consequently, he found himself wanting to remind students about classroom expectations. When he asked her about this, Crystal told him that she was unwilling to be a "bad guy."

> K: I was going to commend you for redirecting her to doing what she should have been doing.
>
> C: Really?
>
> K: I think it's necessary. The kids may get mad at you. If they do, they will get over it quickly. Most of the time, they're really mad at themselves for making a mistake.

On the way home from school that day, Kevin reflected on his work with Crystal. He wondered if his advice early in the year had been the reason Crystal was so concerned with the relationships she had with her students. From the first day they met, he told her that he thought that relationships are the biggest keys to success in a classroom. This included teacher-teacher relationships, teacher-parent relationships, teacher-student relationships, and student-student relationships. He wondered if she thought that the relationships had to be conflict free all the time. Did she think that quality relationships never experienced conflict? He struggled to figure out how to put these pieces together.

As the year continued, Crystal began observing Kevin in his classroom when her students were at specials. She was inquiring into her question of how to correct student behavior in a way she felt was appropriate. She began to notice that students responded differently to Kevin than they did to her. When she led small groups or taught whole group mini-lessons, she experienced a lot of problems with managing students. The students frequently interrupted, grabbed her as she walked by, made inappropriate comments, and in general did not meet her behavior expectations. Kevin experienced these behaviors, but far less frequently than Crystal. In a postconference that followed the observation, Crystal shared her notes and her emerging insights into how to manage both positive student relationships and discipline. Through conversation, dialogue, and observation, Crystal had begun to identify the missing piece. Kevin had to help her figure out where it fit. Crystal never did stop worrying about upsetting the students. She did seem to begin to understand there was more to teaching than making the students happy. Sometimes, we as mentors need to remember that as well—there's more to mentoring than making your mentee feel happy.

SUMMARY

Mentoring is a complex endeavor. Every mentor and mentee is different. Consequently, every mentor-mentee relationship is different. If a mentor is a jigsaw puzzle enthusiast, that mentor will . . .

1. discover the pieces of the puzzle created by the current teaching context (e.g., the connect/disconnect between his own and his mentee's teaching philosophy and practice, the learning climate, the needs of the current student population).

2. craft a plan for putting the pieces together.

3. enact that plan and evaluate it. If the pieces do not fit, it may be necessary to revisit Step 3.

4. constantly search for new puzzle pieces.

5. understand that each new puzzle has entirely different pieces. No two completed puzzles will ever appear the same, nor should they.

For Discussion

1. Tina was a first-year teacher who was extremely talented. When one is mentoring a talented novice, it's easy not to notice any "missing pieces" to their teaching puzzle. What are some strategies you might use as a mentor teacher of a talented novice to find the missing puzzle pieces?

2. Kevin is currently mentoring four novice teachers—Tina, Joseph, Margaret, and Crystal—all at the same time on top of his own teaching load. While we hear in the story how Kevin puts the pieces of each mentee's learning-to-teach puzzle together, we do not know how Kevin fits his own classroom teaching responsibilities into the puzzle. How might a jigsaw puzzle enthusiast cope if he finds out he is working on too many puzzles simultaneously and can't seem to complete any of them?

3. What might you do if you feel as though you are missing a piece of the puzzle? How might you discover what thinking guides your mentee's teaching?

4. What might you do if sometimes the puzzle pieces do not seem to fit? When, if ever, do you think events might require the mentor to force the puzzle pieces together?

(Continued)

(Continued)

5. What would you do if you felt that your mentee was working on a completely different puzzle than you were? In other words, what could you do if you feel as though you and your mentee are incompatible?

6. What components of effective mentoring (creating an educative mentoring context, guiding a mentee's professional knowledge development, and nurturing the development of a mentee's professional dispositions) are evident in this metaphor?

7. List the strengths and limitations of conceptualizing mentoring using a jigsaw puzzle enthusiast metaphor.

8. Regardless of your own mentoring context, what can you learn from this story to inform your own mentoring practice?

5

Mentor as Tailor

The Case of Robin

With Jennifer Jacobs

THE MENTOR

Robin, an African American, first-/second-grade multiage classroom teacher at a university K–12 laboratory school, taught elementary school for fifteen years and subsequently returned to college where she received her doctorate in early childhood education. After she completed her doctorate, Robin taught at the college level and supervised preservice teachers in their field placements. After five years teaching and supervising preservice teachers, Robin decided that it was time to try her hand at teaching children once again, so she took a position teaching primary grades at the university's laboratory school. In this way, she could teach both children and prospective teachers simultaneously.

As a classroom teacher, Robin's goal is to "help kids feel really good about themselves and become motivated, self-directed learners."

Due to her early childhood education background, Robin is very concerned about attending to the whole child. This means that academics are important for learning, but so is the child's emotional and social growth. Robin believes strongly in individualizing instruction and not assuming that each child in her classroom needs the same exact support.

THE MENTEE

Diane, a 21-year-old White female, always wanted to be a teacher and subsequently enrolled in a teacher education program at a major university immediately following her graduation from high school. Diane entered Robin's classroom at the start of her fifth year of a teacher education program that would result in her obtaining a master's degree. Diane had completed all elements of her teacher education coursework with flying colors during the first four years of her program, and was awarded a bachelor's degree midway through this yearlong internship. Eager to begin the final components of her program, Diane was known by her professors as a strong student with a great deal of confidence and wonderful potential for teaching.

THE CONTEXT

Diane joined Robin in her first-/second-grade multiage classroom during the fifth year of her teacher education program to complete a yearlong internship. Unlike many field experiences that follow the university's calendar, in this field experience, interns adopted the calendar of the laboratory school. Diane began working with Robin during preplanning to set up the classroom and stayed until the last day of school. During the fall semester, Diane cotaught in Robin's classroom with another intern each morning and completed methods coursework in the afternoon. The focus of this semester was accommodating diverse learners in the classroom. When the spring semester started, Diane became the sole intern in the classroom for the entire school day. During this semester, Diane's coursework consisted of writing and teaching a curriculum unit and engaging in teacher inquiry about a specific wondering related to her teaching practice. Diane also was responsible for a great deal of the planning, teaching, and attending of grade-level team and school meetings, as well as assessing student learning. Consequently, Diane spent an entire year teaching and learning alongside her mentor teacher.

THE METAPHOR: A TAILOR

According to Webster's Online Dictionary (n.d.), a tailor is a person whose occupation entails the making or altering of garments. The actions of a tailor include accommodating, adjusting, or adapting garments. Just as a tailor adjusts a garment to suit the individual specifications or needs of a customer, as a mentor, Robin makes adjustments to accommodate Diane's individual needs and learning style as she learns to teach. In order to suit the customer's body type and style, the tailor may ask questions such as, "Is this skirt too long for the social event?" "How short should I hem your pants?" or "Does your waist feel comfortable in these trousers?" Similarly, Robin uses reflective questioning to gauge Diane's comfort level regarding teaching responsibilities and emotional well-being. This questioning, or what Robin calls "checking in," helps Robin monitor Diane's growth and make adjustments to Diane's internship experiences. Diane's answers to questions help Robin decide when Diane is ready to take more control and how much scaffolding, or support, she needs. Just as the tailor makes sure each garment is a perfect fit for the customer, Robin creates a context for learning to teach that is a "perfect fit" for her intern Diane.

Much like a tailor, who allows the customer to select the desired clothing article, Robin provides Diane with a great deal of freedom to choose creative lessons and make classroom decisions. She cannot remember ever saying no to any of Diane's ideas for the classroom, believing the only way you really learn whether or not something works is by trying it on your own. However, Robin does not let Diane haphazardly make decisions or plan lessons. Robin sees her mentor role as making sure she supports Diane's learning by adapting, adjusting, and accommodating the support she provides Diane as she expands her professional knowledge. Questioning Diane is not only used to monitor her well-being and comfort level, but is also important to support the growth of her pedagogical thinking. Just as a tailor ask questions such as, "How formal is the event you plan to attend in this outfit?" "What length of skirt is appropriate to wear for a business conference?" or "Should I let out the length of these pants in case she grows any taller?" Robin uses reflective questioning to provoke Diane's reflection about her planning and instructional decisions both before and after teaching. Therefore, Diane can have support, but freedom as well.

The point to remember with the tailor metaphor for mentoring is that just because someone has the freedom to choose and buy his or her own clothes, it does not necessarily mean those clothes will fit. In the same way, endless freedom in the classroom does not mean that learning and growth will automatically occur. A tailor must work with the individual dimensions and preferences of the customer when altering items of clothing. In the case of a tailor's work with a wedding party, the tailor must meet the needs of both the bride and the bridesmaids. Similarly, the mentor must balance the needs of both the novice and the children in the novice's care. Robin realizes that at times there must be pressure with accompanied support to make the tailor's work just right. Helping Diane see dissonance as a source of growth is essential to her development. As a final note, if Robin told her story next year after having another intern, it might sound quite different than her story of mentoring Diane. The experience would be expected to be responsive and based on the individual intern, and therefore different.

A GLIMPSE AT ROBIN, DIANE, AND THE TAILOR METAPHOR IN ACTION

Diane and Robin sit down to meet on Friday afternoon after a very hectic school week in January. Diane has been in the classroom since August, but this is the first month she is no longer coteaching with another student intern. Therefore, she is taking on more teaching responsibilities each day.

Robin begins the conversation, "Wow, what a week! These students truly surprise me each day with the unique things they say or do! You never know what they are going to do next. How did you feel the week went?"

Diane replies, "I was really happy with all my lesson ideas. However, I'm still a little worried about classroom management as I try to implement more hands-on, active lessons. In a few of my lessons, the students seemed to get a little wild and way too loud. Did you see Sammy jumping up and down on the chair because he was so excited about getting to be the cashier for our classroom store in math? The noise just seemed to escalate from there. Don't get me wrong, though, I am so happy you have given me freedom to try my own ideas. I love being able to experiment with new ideas!"

Robin responds, "Yes, you are so creative with your ideas and I feel very confident to let you go ahead and try whatever you wish. I feel that you can never learn unless you try on your own. However, I do share your concern about some issues you are having in classroom management. Sometimes the more complicated your lessons become, the more time you need to spend thinking about management. You need to think through how you are going to hand out materials, expectations for behavior, how you will share those expectations, consequences for behavior, procedures to be used, how you plan to group students, how to move students through transitions, and how you will know what the students learned. Are you sitting down and thinking through the lesson and visualizing what you will do before you teach? How can I support you so this management is not such an issue?"

Diane replies, "I'm trying to think through everything, but a lot of times I totally miss something that is important. Like in the math lesson for which I created the class store, I didn't set any limits on how much money they could start with, so the children began taking handfuls and handfuls of money."

Robin then suggests, "Maybe if we sit down together before the lesson so you can talk through the lesson, I can help prompt you to think about different areas for management reflection. Sometimes it helps if someone is actually asking you those questions about expectations, procedures, consequences, et cetera. Would the afternoon on the day before you teach the lesson give you enough time?"

Diane responds, "That's a wonderful idea! Let's try that! Thinking aloud with you before the lesson will really help me prepare for and reflect on what I plan to do."

Robin moves on, "So this week, you have added teaching science to your current responsibilities of teaching two reading groups, taking students to specials and lunch, and morning meeting. So how are you feeling about these responsibilities? Do you feel overwhelmed?"

Diane responds, "I'm feeling quite good. It's so exciting to teach science because it lends itself to hands-on lessons. I love being creative! And by the way, I have an idea for a lesson about the human body next week. I was thinking that I could go to the supermarket butcher and get a cow heart to bring into the classroom. What do you think?"

Robin pauses for a moment, "Wow, the kids would love that. Tell me more about what you are planning to do."

Diane begins to explain, "I thought about bringing in the heart so the students can begin to think about what a real organ would look like. They usually think a heart resembles what you receive chocolate in for Valentine's Day. I was thinking I would have students sit on the carpet in the front of the room and then hold up the heart. The students could share words to describe the heart and predict the function of the various parts. Then I want to put the heart at one of the organ centers so students could look at it more closely and sketch it."

Robin replies, "I think the cow heart idea is very doable and will be so exciting and motivating for the children. However, let's think it through together. Let me pose some questions that you should think about during the weekend, and then we can talk about this again on Monday after you've solidified a plan. Have you thought about how that is going to work with 24 kids? How you might want to organize the lesson so the kids don't start bouncing off the walls? What do you know about the heart as an organ and a cow heart specifically? How can you make sure they focus on the concepts and relate to the human body instead of just being consumed with the fact that the heart is gross? What possible problems do you think could occur when you put the heart at a center? What behavioral consequences will you have for students who may not follow the parameters you put in place?"

Diane sighs, "You're right; I have not thought about those questions at all. This weekend I am going to plan it out with more details, and then it would be great if I could go through it with you on Monday."

"Sounds great!" Robin replies.

Robin then says, "Before we head home for the weekend, I wanted to check in with you. When do you want to take the lead teaching math full-time? Do you feel that you want to try it, or do you want me to continue leading?"

Diane responds, "Well, at the moment, I would like to spend a week or two more with my current responsibilities. I would find it beneficial to watch you plan and coteach math with you some more, and then I will be ready."

Robin says, "Okay, how about if you plan with me during the next week and then you can lead our coteaching. Would you be comfortable with that?"

"Sure, that's okay," says Diane.

Robin probes Diane a little further, "Are you a little nervous about teaching math because of being overwhelmed with so much responsibility, or are you uncomfortable teaching mathematics concepts?"

Diane shares, "I'm a little nervous about differentiating in mathematics because so many students are at different levels and the fear of not having a math textbook in first grade."

Robin replies, "How about we focus our coplanning on differentiation and places to get ideas for differentiated lessons?"

Diane sighs, "That would make me feel so much better. If I get started with your support and start feeling comfortable, then I'm sure I will feel better about taking the lead in math."

Robin shares, "Also, remember that 'taking something over' doesn't mean we can't talk about your ideas and plans together."

Then Robin begins talking to Diane about how impressed she is with the activities she has planned for her reading group. Robin says, "I am so impressed with the integrated activities you are planning for your reading group. The students seemed so engaged while role-playing different versions of the three little pigs and then getting a chance to write their own story. Can you believe reading was the one subject you were most worried about teaching?"

Diane replies, "No. I'm sure glad that you made me start teaching reading first. I thought it was weird when you asked me what I was least comfortable teaching and then made me start with that."

Robin replies, "If you wait to start your least comfortable subject until the end, then you get the least practice! Okay, well, is there anything else you want to talk about? Do you have any concerns? I want to make sure you are feeling comfortable."

Diane says, "I feel great now, but I will probably have more questions after I plan during the weekend."

Robin states, "Remember, we can check in with each other Monday about what you've planned. I especially am excited to hear about your lesson with the cow heart. Now, let's talk about what you're doing this weekend for fun!"

Like a tailor, Robin's work with Diane requires ongoing adjustments and accommodations that can only be determined if open lines of communication exist between the mentor and the novice. By making sure she has all of Diane's measurements, Robin is able to pull the appropriate tool out of her mentoring toolbox to support Diane's professional growth.

SUMMARY

Mentoring is a complex endeavor. Every mentor and mentee is different. Consequently, every mentor-mentee relationship is different. If a mentor is a tailor, that mentor will . . .

1. assess the "clothes" (mentee's individual needs and learning style) that the mentee enters the teaching profession wearing.

2. ask questions of the mentee to assess the mentee's comfort with teaching responsibilities and emotional well-being.

3. adjust and alter the mentee's experiences to suit the mentee's comfort level.

For Discussion

1. Tailors make alterations to garments (length, waist, etc.) based on their client's body size and shape and fit preferences. What are some alterations you might make in your approach to mentoring if your mentee

- has trouble with classroom management?
- is particularly strong in content knowledge?
- is shy and takes little initiative?
- plans very creative lessons?
- is finding difficulty balancing personal and professional life?

2. As a tailor balances making suggestions to clients about current fashion with the clients' own preferences for length and fit, as a mentor, Robin balances giving her mentee freedom to develop and learn with being sure major concepts and strategies that need to be covered are given appropriate attention. What are some considerations you must take into account as a mentor teacher to balance mentee freedom with meeting goals and objectives each week?

---

3. Diane was a strong beginning teacher. How might the "adjustments" Robin makes to her mentoring practice as a tailor be different if her mentee...

- struggled with lesson planning?
- was unable to manage the classroom?
- was unable to tie assessment of student learning to the goals and objectives of a lesson?

4. Robin's mentee did not feel compelled to use every idea that she gave her. Discuss what your own thoughts and feeling might be if your mentee did not incorporate any of your suggestions into his or her teaching. As a tailor, what adjustments might you make to your mentoring?

5. What components of effective mentoring (creating an educative mentoring context, guiding a mentee's professional knowledge development, nurturing the development of a mentee's professional dispositions) are evident in this metaphor?

6. List the strengths and limitations of conceptualizing mentoring using a tailor metaphor.

7. Regardless of your own mentoring context, what can you learn from this story to inform your own mentoring practice?

6

Mentor as Coach

The Case of Tracy

With Tracy Norman

THE MENTOR

Tracy, a White female, is in her seventh year of teaching. She currently teaches third grade at an inclusion model elementary school where more than 80 percent of the children are African American and receive free or reduced lunch. Tracy is enrolled in a doctoral program at the local university, focusing on supervision. Five years ago, Tracy completed a clinical educator program designed by the county and has been a mentor teacher ever since.

Tracy takes great pride in being repeatedly asked to mentor preservice teachers. She describes her own internship as a preservice teacher, through the university, as not a particularly supportive learning experience. She had to learn to become a reflective practitioner on her own, while planning lessons and designing assessment. She believes in inclusive teaching and differentiated instruction, and is committed to building a positive classroom community. That less-than-positive experience from her own internship is what spurred her interest in mentoring students from the university teacher education program, and her willingness to take on a new mentoring responsibility this year. In an effort to recruit and retain teachers in this high-need, high-poverty school, Tracy's district has initiated a new apprentice program, in which veteran teachers share their classrooms with an apprentice for the entire year. Based on her prior experience mentoring university teacher education students, in this new apprentice program, Tracy believes in creating an environment where she and her apprentice feel comfortable trying new things without worrying about what mistakes they might make. In addition, Tracy wishes to foster her own and her apprentice's reflection throughout the school year based on observation data and student learning data that they collaboratively explore.

THE MENTEE

Jen, Tracy's apprentice, met with Tracy during the summer to get acquainted and discuss the setup of their soon-to-be shared classroom. Jen was young, energetic, and very bright. She had majored in English in college, and had graduated summa cum laude. During her study abroad in Scotland during her senior year, she decided that she wanted to pursue teaching, following in her mother's footsteps. Her mom, a special education teacher, had dedicated her life to working with hard-to-reach students. Not exactly sure what to do with her English degree, Jen decided she wanted to devote her life to children, just as her mother had. She explored Teach for America and even went to an interview to become a part of this program targeted at teaching in challenging urban schools. When she heard about the apprenticeship program, however, she decided to take this route to teaching.

Tracy was impressed with the knowledge Jen brought to the apprenticeship, which was based on observing and talking with her mother through the years. Jen was willing to meet prior to school starting to talk about classroom management, teaching philosophies, and how the inclusion model worked at the school. When the two began the school year during preplanning, they already knew a lot about each other and felt comfortable dialoguing together.

In their discussion, Jen quickly voiced her commitment to student learning and interest in building a strong classroom community with engaging instruction. She planned to engage the students in activities that highlighted diversity, conflict resolution, and working together for a better world. Typical of novice teachers, Jen's fear was classroom management, and she hoped that, with tweaking, that would improve dramatically throughout the year.

THE CONTEXT

Jen entered Tracy's classroom as part of an alternative certification apprenticeship. She spent every day of a complete school year in the classroom with Tracy and received the stipend of a paraprofessional. Following her apprentice year, Jen would be assigned her own class-room of students. The apprenticeship was designed to have new, nontraditionally prepared teachers work closely with master teachers while engaging in alternative preparation coursework and online modules. The apprenticeship model relied on Jen's observations of Tracy and Tracy's coaching in the areas of lesson design, implementation, assessment of student learning, classroom management, and all the other responsibilities related to teaching. In addition to Tracy's support, Jen's principal evaluated her teaching on a monthly basis, offering feedback and suggestions. Additionally, she attended district workshops for certification preparation.

Throughout the year, Jen and Tracy engaged in a coteaching model, where they both directed the students and circulated through-out the classroom interchangeably. On many occasions, this led to reflection-in-action as they examined student work and made adjustments during instruction, and reflection-on-action as they reviewed the students' work and set goals accordingly for the next day. Jen's maturity and willingness to try new things, and Tracy's openness and their shared interest in student learning, allowed for this kind of environment to exist.

Tracy's school had also begun to use teacher inquiry, defined as systematic, intentional study of teachers' own classroom practice, as a tool for professional development focused on student learning (Dana & Yendol-Silva, 2003). Given the demographics of Tracy and Jen's school as well as the high-stakes accountability system that seems to guide much decision making, at the start of the school year,

Tracy and Jen focused their inquiry on a shared wondering: "How do we enhance student engagement, on-task behavior, and student learning in a high-poverty school where high-stakes accountability has shifted instruction toward the test?"

THE METAPHOR: A COACH

Tracy's work with Jen assumed the role of a coach. In this case, a coach is a person who provides specific targeted instruction or support to enhance performance. The coaches of athletic teams watch their players' development, talk to their players about their perceptions of the game and individual skills, practice and put into play new strategies and techniques, watch film of games to better understand the needs of the team and individual players, talk with players based on what was learned from analyzing film, and begin the cycle again. Similarly, Tracy uses a reflective coaching cycle she learned about in her clinical education training to "coach" Jen's development as a teacher.

The reflective coaching cycle is described as "a multistage cycle that includes establishing readiness, a pre-conference, the teaching observation, analysis of the data, a post-observation conference and an overall evaluation of the process" (Nolan & Hoover, 2005). In Step 1, establishing readiness, the mentor and novice teacher share with each other their beliefs about teaching and learning within a context of trust and support. In Step 2, the preconference, the novice teacher identifies an area of inquiry that she would like to explore within the lesson she will be teaching. The power of the preconference is that it allows the novice teacher to guide the mentor's gaze to an area of perceived need or felt difficulty and the two collaboratively decide the type of data to be collected in the observation. Once the novice and the mentor enter Step 3, the teaching observation, the mentor captures the agreed-upon data and other anecdotes related to the inquiry focus. Upon completion of the observation, the mentor and the novice teacher engage in a postconference, Step 4, which includes the collaborative analysis of the data, dialogue about the meaning and implications of the data, and goal setting for future teaching efforts. At this point, the cycle repeats itself.

In addition to a commitment to reflective coaching, Jen and Tracy began talking during preplanning. Tracy noticed that Jen seemed to voice concern about student engagement and student learning. Thus, Tracy identified that as her first targeted area of instruction and support. As a result, Tracy and Jen discussed many ideas that involved teaching strategies, subject matter, student manipulatives, and student knowledge attainment that Jen could try out during their year together. They hoped, through coaching, Jen would be able to enhance her students' performance. As a mentor, Tracy knew through coaching she could provide the opportunities and support for Jen to try new things and gain insight into how she might better engage students.

A GLIMPSE OF TRACY, JEN, AND THE COACH METAPHOR IN ACTION

On a hot, sunny day in late July, Tracy and Jen met for lunch at a local diner. They had already been introduced at a school function for all district apprentices and their mentors the prior week, and were anxious to get to know each other better and begin to plan for the year ahead. During lunch, Tracy and Jen shared a little bit with each other about their personal lives, and what brought them each to a career in teaching. Intrigued by Jen's mixed excitement and trepidation about teaching in a high-poverty school and joining the new apprentice program, Tracy queried Jen about some of her ideas about the career she was about to begin:

"So, tell me Jen, you seem to be really passionate about teaching high-poverty kids. What do you think good teaching of high-poverty kids would look like?"

Jen replied, "I remember so much of school as being boring— 'drill and kill' was how I affectionately referred to many of my school experiences. I think it's really important to engage learners. The things I liked most about my school experiences were the things we did, not worksheets—I want the students to be engaged and have fun. I've also watched my mom teach for years. She's really dedicated to helping kids that are struggling with learning. I've seen her spend hours making manipulatives to teach these kids. I think engaging kids is really important!"

Tracy responded, "I agree that it is important to engage students and have fun, but you know, as a teacher in a high-poverty school, you are under a lot of pressure to prepare students for the state assessment test. If they don't pass in third grade, they'll be retained!

Some drill and practice through worksheets might be just what a student needs to pass this test. As a teacher who shares your belief that learning should be engaging, I've been struggling a bit with finding the balance between responding to pressure to prepare students for the state test and teaching in ways that are engaging to students. This is something you can help me think about a little more this year as you become more familiar with the curriculum, the context, and teaching."

Jen and Tracy's conversation continued through lunch, with Tracy asking Jen multiple questions that led to great discussion, such as, "Tell me a little bit about the ways you believe kids learn best" and "What are your biggest fears about teaching?" Through the discussion that occurred on this hot summer day and numerous other similar dialogues they engaged in before, during, and after school, Tracy and Jen developed a mutual trust, rapport, and respect for each other.

In October, after two months of teaching together, Jen began to take on more responsibility for the planning of lessons for their classroom. Tracy noticed rather quickly that Jen's classroom management techniques and style of teaching didn't always keep students' attention and that they both continued to have questions about student learning. Tracy believed it was time to move into the next phase of the coaching cycle—the preconference.

"Jen, you've been learning a lot teaching alongside me over these first couple of months of the school year, and I'm proud of the way you are beginning to plan your own lessons in math. I know the principal will be doing her first apprentice observation and evaluation of you next month. To help you get used to observation, I'd like to make sure that I 'officially' observe one of your lessons per week. Unlike the one you will have with the principal, my observations will not be evaluative. Instead, my observations will be targeted at helping you think more about your teaching and student learning. Let's have a conference before and after each observation. When we conference before the observation, we can agree on what questions you want to explore about your own teaching during that lesson and the ways I might collect some data for you that could give you insights into your questions after the lesson is taught. We also will want to look at student work from the lesson, so let's be sure to have that with us at the postconference. We can look at that data together."

Reflecting on this process, Jen told Tracy, "I feel more confident already. During the time of the observations, I hope that I see more student engagement and on-task behavior while at the same time gain a better understanding of student learning. This is something I feel I really need to work on. I am comfortable with you observing me because you are easy to talk to, and you give feedback that I can use."

Two days later, Tracy and Jen engaged in their first preconference before school around a lesson Jen was going to teach on mixed numbers that afternoon. Tracy started the preconference by asking Jen which math skills she planned to teach, what the lesson objectives included, what data should be collected, what materials she would need, and what the student work would look like. Tracy knew that as a coach she would need to give Jen the freedom to choose how she would teach the lesson and then sit back and capture data that would allow her to see how she did. The preconference established that Tracy would use a seating chart to collect data on students' engagement in the lesson on mixed numbers and student work to identify the degree of student learning.

At lunch that day, Jen reflected on the preconference with another apprentice in the building who was interested in how Jen's day was going:

> Tracy and I sat down for a preconference this morning to review a lesson plan I created for teaching mixed numbers. She questioned and reassured my ideas and activities to make sure that we were on target with the learning outcomes we had previously discussed. We completed a walk-through, and she helped me determine what examples to start with and what aspects of the lesson the students may have trouble understanding. I found this preconference to be very helpful, and I will go into the lesson this afternoon confident in my ideas and activities. I feel that the preconference allowed me to ask any questions I had about the lesson and gain an additional perspective on the lesson. In addition, Tracy gave me helpful hints and tips to try.

After lunch, Jen eagerly began her lesson on mixed numbers. Tracy sat next to a student, observing and keeping track of on-task behavior using a seating chart of the class. At five-minute intervals,

Tracy did a sweep of the entire classroom and noted on the seating chart of the class the behavior of each learner using a key: "A" represented active listening, "ON" represented on-task behavior, and "OT" represented off-task behavior.

Jen was ready for the postconference observation after school and arrived with the pile of student work and anecdotes she had noted during the lesson. During the postconference, Tracy began by asking questions about how Jen thought the lesson had gone and what changes she would make in the future. Tracy didn't want to come right out and tell Jen what she thought should change. Rather, Jen's self-reflection was what Tracy was interested in hearing. The conversation naturally shifted to the data collected as Tracy and Jen looked at the chart to see at what point in the lesson students were most engaged. They also analyzed the student work for concept attainment. When Jen interpreted the data, she realized that when she used math manipulatives, the students were highly engaged and attained the concepts at the concrete level. However, they still had difficulties moving to the more abstract use of the concept, as evidenced in the student work she collected. This led to further questions related to concept attainment and students' application of knowledge that they agreed to explore in the next coaching cycle.

When Tracy and Jen were finished with the postconference, Tracy asked Jen about her experience with the coaching cycle. She told Tracy that the process made her feel more prepared for the lesson. As Jen reflected, she mentioned that the discussion about student work reminded her that she needed to be clear about the conceptual knowledge of the math content herself. She wanted to spend more time thinking about how to translate the math content into instruction that would support their shift to the abstract. Additionally, the cycle allowed her to feel as if they were working more closely together on both her teaching development and student learning. She was being coached rather than evaluated or judged.

As the cycles progressed, Jen and Tracy collaboratively explored many new pedagogical approaches to math using manipulatives and materials, including fraction blocks, unifix cubes, white boards and dry erase markers, and math journals. These strategies became new regularities in the classroom as both Tracy and Jen recognized their merit based on the student learning that they had witnessed, and embraced them.

The data that was collected through each coaching cycle were also beneficial for their collaborative teacher inquiry into enhancing student engagement and learning in a high-poverty school where high-stakes accountability shifted instruction toward the test. The data they gathered led Jen and Tracy to better understand how their students experienced multiple learning activities and how their experiences translated to their attitudes about school and performance on the state test. Tracy and Jen shared their learning about student engagement with colleagues at a faculty meeting at the end of the school year.

SUMMARY

Mentoring is a complex endeavor. Every mentor and mentee is different. Consequently, every mentor-mentee relationship is different. If a mentor is a coach, that mentor will . . .

1. establish a trusting relationship with the mentee, with the understanding that an established trusting relationship capitalizes on the mentee's ability to be responsive to coaching sessions.

2. select and target particular lessons for coaching.

3. engage mentees in a preconference before the selected lesson for observation. Likened to an athletic coach giving his or her team a pregame talk, in the preconference, a mentor leads the mentee in a review of the goal of the lesson and the strategies and tactics to be used in the lesson, and helps the mentee visualize how the lesson (or "game") will play out.

4. select data-collection strategies that will help the mentee gain insights into his or her teaching and collects this data during the teaching act, a process similar to the athletic coach who collects data during a game by filming and noting statistics.

5. meet with the mentee after the lesson to review and analyze the collected data, drawing conclusions about teaching and learning to be put into play in future lessons.

For Discussion

1. The coaching cycle that Tracy and Jen engage in numerous times during the school year is extremely time intensive—requiring approximately a one-hour meeting prior to a lesson being taught and another one-hour (or more) meeting after the lesson is taught. It is best if these meetings occur as close to the act of teaching as possible. Given that each teaching day is already overbooked, what are some ways a mentor and mentee can find time to engage in pre- and postconferencing?

2. Athletic coaches understand their players' psyches and use this knowledge to make decisions about when to push players and when their players require rest. You are working with a mentee who just completed a lesson she obviously worked on and planned for hours. In your postconference, she is bubbling about how successful she believed her lesson to be because 25 out of the 27 students in the class performed well on the assessment she gave at the close of the lesson. How and when might you "push" this intern to consider the two children who did not perform well on the assessment without "bursting her bubble?"

3. The foundation for the coaching cycle is the development of mutual respect between mentor and mentee, and the establishment of a collaborative working relationship. To establish this relationship, oftentimes a mentor and mentee's professional and personal lives begin to intertwine with one another. What do you do if . . .

- you are assigned to work with a mentee who is doing well professionally but your personalities clash?
- you and your mentee become personal friends and the comfort and familiarity you have established with each other leads your mentee to behave in ways that aren't professional?
- you feel hurt when your mentee, an extremely private person, continues to turn down your attempts to develop your relationship through such venues as coming to your home for a dinner or stopping for a cup of coffee after work?

4. What might you do if your mentee has trouble naming an area he or she wishes you to focus on during your preconference?

5. What components of effective mentoring (creating an educative mentoring context, guiding a mentee's professional knowledge development, and nurturing the development of a mentee's professional dispositions) are evident in this metaphor?

6. List the strengths and limitations of conceptualizing mentoring using a coach metaphor.

7. Regardless of your own mentoring context, what can you learn from this story to inform your own mentoring practice?

7

Mentor as Mirror

The Case of Claudia

THE MENTOR

Claudia, a 47-year-old White female, is in her fourteenth year of teaching first-grade children. She did not start out as an education major. After getting her undergraduate degree in psychology and philosophy, Claudia went back to the university for a one-year intensive master of arts in teaching program, coupled with a full year teaching in the university lab school. Her training within the lab school was a setting similar to today's professional development schools, as it was an innovative school-university partnership designed around the notion of simultaneous renewal for prospective and practicing teachers as well as teacher educators. Claudia believes her own mentor teacher was excellent because she provided a supportive and caring context for teaching. Claudia's own positive preservice teaching experience contributed to her interest in working with prospective teachers, and she draws upon memories of her own mentor teacher and learning-to-teach experiences as she mentors new teachers in the professional development school.

As a classroom teacher, Claudia is committed to providing a context and stimulus for children to construct knowledge actively. She uses child-centered pedagogy such as cooperative learning, conflict resolution, peer tutoring, and student problem solving as daily instructional techniques. According to Claudia, building a strong professional relationship with her mentee is a necessary component of her mentoring, and she explains, "I really feel that Julia and I have a much closer relationship personally and professionally because we really spend a lot of time dialoguing together. It is more intimate, so to speak, because you are together so much."

THE MENTEE

Julia, Claudia's intern, is a capable, bright, reflective, and energetic 21-year-old woman. As with many prospective teachers, she has struggled a bit with classroom management, but overall she is strong and well planned in her work with children. Additionally, Julia has really refined observational skills and she is very reflective. She does a lot of question asking, and she has a real curiosity about her teaching; she always wants to know why. One of the most interesting characteristics of Julia is that she holds certain beliefs that she really sticks to and doesn't succumb to going back into the traditional mode when things get tough. This has been a real asset in the current context of accountability that pressures teachers to teach to the test regardless of their own beliefs about how children learn.

THE CONTEXT

Julia enters Claudia's first-grade classroom as a preservice teacher within a professional development school where Julia will complete her undergraduate internship by teaming with Claudia for an entire school year. Claudia and Julia share many philosophical beliefs and a level of commitment to these beliefs. A certain "telepathy" often exists between the two of them because they think a lot alike. In addition to teaching alongside Claudia, Julia engages in seminars and coursework conducted at her school site. Julia's teacher education program departs from the traditional initial teacher preparation program in three important ways. First, Claudia and Julia team-teach children throughout an *entire* school year. Second, Claudia works closely with Julia's methods instructors. Third, Claudia and Julia engage in collaborative teacher inquiry throughout the year.

THE METAPHOR: A MIRROR

A mirror is defined as "a surface such as glass or polished metal that reflects light without diffusing it so that it will give back a clear image of anything placed in front of it" (Webster's Online Dictionary, n.d.). In the context of education, Schön (1983) describes two types of reflection: *reflection on action* occurs after an action as a way of thinking about a completed lesson; *reflection in action* occurs during a lesson. For reflection to occur, the teacher must recreate an image of himself or herself as the teaching act is unfolding, thoughtfully consider that image, and take action and make adjustments in teaching based on the image he or she is seeing.

A verb that is commonly associated with the noun *mirror* is *reflect*. In the context of a mirror, to reflect is to redirect something that strikes a surface, especially light, sound, or heat, back toward its point of origin. As Claudia mentors Julia into the teaching profession, she often serves as a mirror for Julia, helping Julia "see" a clear image of her own teaching or "reflecting" Julia's questions back to her for further exploration. Additionally, Claudia often commits to "mirroring" the methods coursework for the interns in her school.

A GLIMPSE OF CLAUDIA, JULIA, AND THE MIRROR METAPHOR IN ACTION

Claudia and Julia began the year coteaching during preplanning. The children wouldn't start school for another week, so Claudia and Julia got to know each other as they set up their classroom. Their ability to communicate from the onset facilitated Claudia's ability to develop the mirror metaphor and helped deepen Julia's teaching practice. The following five scenarios give you glimpses into their school year together and how various aspects of the mirror metaphor unfolded.

Glimpse 1—Reflecting to Redirect Julia Back to Her Teaching

Claudia and Julia sat down after school one day early in the year to reflect on the events of the afternoon. It had been a particularly challenging afternoon for Julia because of issues of classroom management. Claudia could tell that Julia was having trouble setting expectations for her students' behavior. Particularly, Julia was putting a lot of energy into trying to be consistent in her expectations for all of her students. As a result, the set of expectations seemed to meet the needs of the majority of her students but didn't seem to be working for a few of the children, who continued to be disruptive.

Claudia wanted to push Julia's thinking about the events. Given that dialogue and questioning were central to Claudia's mirror metaphor, Claudia began probing Julia with questions that would help her recreate the images of that day's struggles.

Claudia began by asking, "So tell me about how you thought things went this afternoon."

Julia began by describing the events of the lesson: "I guess I had hoped to engage all 22 of the students in the writing activity, and I felt as though I had designed an activity that would allow all of them to be successful at their own level. Many of the students were able to work independently after I had given the directions but not all of them. I found myself getting frustrated with a few of them because the wouldn't stay on task."

"And why were you so frustrated with Mary, Tyran, and Juan's behavior?"

Julia responded, "I thought they could have put more energy into their work and gotten a lot more accomplished."

When Julia had finished sharing, Claudia invited Julia to elaborate on a thought she had previously shared.

"What do you mean by more energy?"

After Julia elaborated on her use of the word *energy*, Claudia rephrased what she heard in Julia's comments: "So I hear you saying that the writing assignment worked great for the majority of our students, but some of our kids need some more scaffolding if they are going to be successful. It sounds as though you think they actually do have the energy but it isn't very directed at the tasks you wish them to complete."

Julia nodded.

"So what might have been the reason behind their behavior and what can we do about it?

Julia paused, "I am not sure, to be honest. Maybe I need to have them sit with me so that I can make sure they remain on task. Or, maybe I need a better consequence for their choice to not complete their work. I am just not sure."

"How did they respond to the writing project?" Claudia asked.

"Well, now that I think about it, Mary seemed to be struggling with the topic. She didn't have many ideas of what to put down on the paper. Tyran and Juan seemed to have ideas, but getting them on paper was the problem."

"What could be the reason that they are having problems getting their ideas on paper?" Claudia inquired.

"Well, I know that two of them struggle with handwriting. One of them likes to be perfect and the other really has difficulties with fine motor coordination. I guess that could be part of the problem. I think maybe I should work on helping Mary concept-map her ideas on paper as a part of her prewriting. That might help Mary get started. . . . And maybe you could help me with some ideas for what to do for students who have handwriting challenges."

"So I hear you saying that in order for these three to be successful, we are going to need to make some specific accommodations and it is our job to figure out what those accommodations will be." Indeed, the focus of most of Julia's initial comments were on herself and what she had done but not on what the students felt and what they may have needed to be successful.

After hearing Claudia's purposeful rephrasing and questioning, Julia was spurred on to reconsider initial thoughts and conclusions that she may have made too hastily in her quest to improve, learn, and grow as a novice teacher.

Glimpse 2—Modeling the Importance of Solo Reflection

On a cool afternoon during the second week of school, Claudia sat down behind her desk after the children had headed off for lunch. She looked thoughtful and relaxed. She was not engaged in the daily paperwork of teaching and seemed available to talk. Julia thought this might be a great time to talk to Claudia about the morning reading groups, as she was curious about how Claudia had processed their morning together and was eager to hear her thoughts. Julia really valued Claudia's efforts to collaboratively reflect with her, and Claudia enjoyed her postlesson dialogue with Julia.

Although lunchtime seemed a logical time to engage in reflective dialogue, when Julia approached Claudia, Claudia acknowledged that she, too, was puzzled by the reading groups and was trying to figure out how to improve the groups for the next day. The dilemma seemed to be that the children were all expected to use the same textbook series but that the reading level of the children within the classroom didn't suggest the series was an appropriate curricular choice. As a result, about a third of the children were frustrated and about a third of the students were bored. In Claudia's mind, only about one-third of the children were getting the appropriate level of instruction. The problem was that the school district insisted that all first graders use the first-grade reading series and that they would be required to turn in the students' scores on the theme test at the end of each unit. Claudia really believed that they needed to provide the struggling students with more fluency work and the advanced learners with more sophisticated vocabulary development opportunities.

However, rather than inviting Julia into co-reflection at that moment, she encouraged Julia to engage in some solo reflection. Claudia shared, "You know, I really needed time to regroup and get my thoughts together after realizing that the curriculum is not working for everyone. I am still on data overload and I don't really have an idea of what to do yet. Let's take some quiet time to gather our individual thoughts. Why don't you do the same and then we can get together after school and brainstorm?"

Through these comments, Claudia reveals to Julia that it is critical for teachers to have space to think about teaching and that this time can be useful for Julia to develop her own reflections before they co-reflect. Besides being legitimately puzzled as to how she was going to negotiate the demands of the curriculum and the needs of her students, Claudia wanted to be sure that Julia wasn't always socialized into her way of thinking. She wanted to honor Julia's independently formed thoughts. Claudia was encouraging Julia to develop her ability to reflect independently.

Glimpse 3—Purposefully Placing Julia Back in the Role of Observer After She Has Done a Considerable Amount of Teaching

A few months into the year Claudia realized that Julia had made tremendous progress in her teaching and was actually quite competent. At first, she thought that her job as a mentor might be done because Julia was already as developed as many first-year teachers. However, on further reflection, she realized her next responsibility was to move Julia beyond the level of competence and to continue developing Julia's knowledge of the complexity of teaching. To these ends, Claudia made the intentional and purposeful decision to pull Julia back from specific teaching responsibilities that she felt comfortable with and place her in the role of observer so that she could reflect back her observations on that specific activity once again. The goal would be for the two of them to exchange assuming the role of mirror on a regular basis in order to encourage even deeper thinking about their pedagogy. Claudia believed that with each exchange, both she and Julia would gain deeper insights into the nuances of their teaching.

The next day, after leading the morning meeting for the last month, Julia returned to observing Claudia lead the morning meeting. Immediately, Julia was surprised at all the new things she noticed that she didn't remember noticing in her earlier observations. During her observation, she noticed particular things that Claudia did as she taught as well as the behaviors and responses of particular children.

When the children went to art class, Julia sat down with Claudia to discuss her new observations from the morning meeting. She noted, "I never realized how much questioning you do related to the calendar and the different types of questions that you ask different children. How do you differentiate your questions? I would like to look at the kinds of questions I ask during morning meeting. I also noticed that a few kids appear to not be paying attention. I am wondering what I can do about that."

Although this action of moving Julia back to the observer seat was antithetical to many student teaching programs where student teachers begin as observers and then slowly take on teaching responsibilities until they successfully "solo" for the final weeks of the semester, Claudia sought to reposition Julia to observer, where she could now become the mirror for Claudia. Because Julia now had experience leading the morning meeting and was less concerned about learning the logistics, the observations provided the opportunity to notice the nuances of the morning meeting. Ultimately, Julia and Claudia engaged in an inquiry into student learning during the morning meeting. Julia and Claudia began to make connections by juxtaposing their ideas about how to strengthen the learning that occurred during morning meeting. This allowed Julia to compare and contrast their approaches and raise questions about her own teaching. This technique created mirrors for both Claudia and Julia that began to push their reflection to a new level, and they began to collaboratively and systematically inquire into their new shared interest.

Glimpse 4—Intentionally Deflecting Questions

Later in the year, as Julia gained more knowledge of the classroom and confidence in her teaching ability, Claudia felt it important to begin removing the scaffolding and support that Julia sometimes relied on. This meant that at times, Claudia needed to make Julia "figure things out for herself." Given their strong relationship, their shared interest in co-reflection, and their daily coteaching, Claudia and Julia had built a practice around constantly dialoguing with one another during the teaching act.

Claudia wanted Julia to see that she could make decisions on her own. Thus, Claudia warned Julia that she would be intentionally and purposefully "refusing" to answer some of the questions Julia faced as she taught.

The next day, during a science lesson, one student, Mary, asked Julia whether she could work with a partner rather than explore a topic alone. Her friend Tamara was interested in the same topic, so it made sense to Mary that they work together. Julia immediately looked to Claudia to get her opinion about the request. Having students work together was something that Claudia and Julia often did in their classroom, but this lesson was specifically designed with an independent assessment that would need altering if the two were to collaborate on the same topic. Additionally, Mary didn't have a particular set of skills needed for a component of the project. This made answering the request more complicated. Claudia felt that Julia was ready to make the decision on her own. So, as Julia looked at Claudia, Claudia just lowered her head, a purposeful ignoring of Julia's gaze. Avoiding eye contact with Julia, she murmured quietly, "It's for you to decide. What do you think?" Claudia's body language and quiet questioning deflected the decision away from her and encouraged Julia to decide independently. In this case, Claudia intentionally chose to use the mentoring mirror to deflect, rather than to reflect.

Glimpse 5—Mirroring Coursework

One of the hallmarks of professional development schools is the commitment of all participants to blend theory and practice. Claudia's mentoring supports this commitment, as she takes pride in her efforts to mirror within her first-grade classroom the methods instruction that Julia is receiving from the university.

Claudia's ability to mirror the methods instruction is made possible by her familiarity with the content of the courses. Claudia serves as a school-based liaison to the math methods course instructor and often meets with the instructor to develop assignments and develop lessons that Julia and her peers can observe.

One day in October, Robert, the math methods course instructor, met Claudia in the hallway at school. He mentioned how frustrated he was that the interns did not seem to see the importance of doing student math interviews with the children in their classrooms. Claudia reminded him that this was probably because the interns hadn't seen a math interview and weren't sure exactly how to do one. As a result, she agreed to have Julia and her peers watch her conduct the math interviews with her students.

During the next two weeks, interns visited Claudia and Julia's classroom in groups of six to ten to observe the interviews. While the interns watched, Claudia sat down with a student and asked general attitudinal questions such as, "Do you like math?" and "Do you think you are good at math?" Then Claudia would pull out the unifix cubes and begin asking the child to demonstrate one-to-one correspondence, moving from the concrete to more conceptual questions. The interview would continue as a type of pre-assessment for each of the skills to be taught in the next few weeks. By the end of the interview, Claudia had a very strong sense of who the child was mathematically and his or her current conceptual knowledge in the areas explored. Additionally, the interns observing now had a good understanding of how a student interview was conducted and how it could be used.

Once all the interns observed Claudia mirror the methods instruction as she taught first graders, Claudia was invited to the methods class. During her visit, Robert asked her to debrief the experience of conducting student interviews by describing the strengths and weaknesses of the process. She then responded to questions from the group. Claudia's willingness to serve as a mirror deepened both her own teaching of mathematics as well as the interns' understanding of teaching mathematics.

SUMMARY

Mentoring is a complex endeavor. Every mentor and mentee is different. Consequently, every mentor-mentee relationship is different. If a mentor is a mirror, that mentor will . . .

1. pose questions about teaching and paraphrase the mentee's responses to questions in order for the mentee to develop a mirror image of a teaching episode. Through further mentee questioning, this mirror image is carefully considered and studied.

2. emphasize and engage in both individual and collaborative reflection.

3. intentionally shift a mentee back from teaching to observing to allow the mentee to see and discover new things about teaching he or she would not have previously discovered based on his or her developmental level. Mentor and mentee question each other after the observation to enable both to develop a mirror image of the teaching episode that they can carefully consider and study together.

4. mirror research-based practices in his or her teaching.

For Discussion

1. To serve as a mirror, helping a mentee recreate an image of himself or herself as teacher during a lesson, mentors need time and space to reflect themselves, as well as dialogue with their mentees. The luxury of time to reflect is rare in the

hectic pace of the school day, with the dual responsibilities of teaching students content and mentees about teaching. What are some considerations mentors should take into account as they struggle to balance time for self-reflection, time for their own students, and time spent reflecting with a mentee?

2. Julia understood and respected her mentor's need for time and space to reflect by herself before they reflected together. What actions might a mentor take if his or her mentee commandeers too much of the mentor's time?

3. To stimulate further growth and reflection in a very competent mentee, toward the end of the school year, you decide to take back the teaching of the subject your mentee excels at delivering, and put your mentee in the role of observer. What do you do when you overhear

   a) your mentee sharing with another beginning teacher that he doesn't understand why you are not letting him teach all day?

   b) two colleagues calling you "crazy" for taking mentoring so seriously when you should be having some "time off from teaching" as your student teacher "solos" during the final days of the semester?

   c) your student teacher's supervisor asking your principal if she was aware of a problem because you are not following the guidelines in the student teaching manual that suggest the student teacher solos during the final weeks of his or her field experience?

4. Claudia's use of the mentor-as-mirror metaphor serves to take Julia's level of self-reflection to deeper levels. As the school year unfolds, Julia takes Claudia's self-reflection to deeper levels as well. This reciprocal mirror relationship becomes a wonderful source of professional growth for Claudia and a benefit of mentoring. What other ways might mentors benefit from the experience of mentoring?

5. What do you do if your mentee is less curious and reflective about teaching than Julia?

6. Could Claudia use this mentoring pedagogy if her beliefs about teaching differed from Julia's substantially? Why? Why not? How?

7. What components of effective mentoring (creating an educative mentoring context, guiding a mentee's professional knowledge development, and nurturing the development of a mentee's professional dispositions) are evident in this metaphor?

8. List the strength and limitations of conceptualizing mentoring using a mirror metaphor.

9. Regardless of your own mentoring context, what can you learn from this story to inform your own mentoring practice?

Mentor as Interior Designer

The Case of Paige

With Angela Gregory

THE MENTOR

Paige, a White 62-year-old woman, was a science teacher and high school principal for 25 years before retiring. She had returned to school while she was teaching to pursue a master's and doctoral degree in curriculum and instruction at a local university. After teaching high school in various contexts and working as a high school principal, Paige retired and was hired by a large urban school district as a part-time mentor of novice teachers.

As a mentor, Paige's goal was to support novice teachers in "navigating the minefields of education" by helping them find ways to link knowledge from their alternative certification coursework and research-based practices to their classroom teaching while still attending to the bureaucratic demands of schools. To guide her mentoring practice, she regularly draws upon her own experiences of learning to teach as well as her work with novices and tenured teachers throughout her career in education. Based on her own professional experiences and challenges, Paige is very conscious of the pervasive disconnect teachers often experience between the "bookwork" or training of learning to teach and the work within a real classroom.

Paige approaches her work with novice teachers much like she did her work with students. She conceives of her role as supporting and guiding the novice through the learning-to-teach process. Her goal is for the novice teachers she works with to construct their own meaning and to help them learn how to apply their own knowledge to new situations through using teachable moments and modeling.

THE MENTEE

Yolanda, a 33-year-old African American woman, enrolled in an alternative teacher certification program in a large school district with a diverse student population. She entered her first classroom assignment after a short career in accounting. She had immediately known that accounting wasn't for her and that she wanted to work with children. As a single mother of two young children, Yolanda was thrilled to hear about the alternative certification program in the city schools that would allow her to receive a paycheck for teaching while simultaneously working toward teacher certification. This seemed like the perfect job, as she would then have the summers off and, she believed, shorter work hours. She believed that this lifestyle would fit well with her role as a mother.

Although Yolanda is very excited about her new career, she is unsure of how to synthesize all the information she is getting from a variety of different sources. She meets regularly with the assistant principal, curriculum support teacher, department head, standards coach, and her mentor. Although it seems like a lot of help, Yolanda is somewhat overwhelmed and is asking her mentor to help her sort out what she needs to do to meet the needs of all the stakeholders involved.

THE CONTEXT

The high school where Yolanda works is beset by many problems, including a decreasing tax base, aging facilities, overcrowded schools, struggling students, and high student mobility, as well as increasing state pressure for higher student test scores. Not surprisingly, this urban district has difficulty recruiting and retaining new teachers. Additionally, Yolanda's school is among the highest need schools in the district. Yolanda teaches mathematics to tenth and twelfth graders, which means she has two class preparations. The department head has asked her to stick closely to the textbook and to be sure to prepare them for the state test. At her school, there is little interaction among the math teachers, as they work rather autonomously. Periodically, the department head and the school standards coach will check on the electronically submitted test data she must submit for each of her students. This is the district's way of monitoring student progress.

THE METAPHOR: AN INTERIOR DESIGNER

Interior design is defined as "the art or practice of planning and supervising the design and execution of architectural interiors and their furnishings" (Webster's Online Dictionary, n.d.). Interior designers begin by consulting with their client to identify a focus based on their client's individual needs. Designers then assess the space before drafting an organizational plan, recommending furnishings, and selecting coordinating materials to enhance the interior. The interior designer can do this by working alone or collaboratively with the client. The interior designer then develops a plan to present to the client that provides various options for furnishings and decorations, which allow the client to refine the proposal to ensure that the plan is in line with his or her personal needs and preferences.

Organizing, accessorizing, and coordinating are common actions associated with interior design. Using the metaphor of interior design in the context of mentoring, the mentor supervises the organization of the design space (i.e., the classroom) by accessorizing the space with appropriate furnishings (i.e., instructional lessons) that meet the needs of the client and their guests (i.e., teacher and students). The space is then enhanced by the selection of coordinating fabrics and décor (i.e., strategies and skills) to make a space functional, inviting, and aesthetically pleasing.

A GLIMPSE OF PAIGE, YOLANDA, AND THE INTERIOR DESIGN METAPHOR IN ACTION

As Paige sat down to get to know her new mentee, Yolanda, many thoughts ran through her head. She thought about the vast set of knowledge and skills related to teaching mathematics that she would need to share with Yolanda as she learned to teach in this challenging inner-city high school. She realized that the responsibility for mentoring novices who lacked substantial teacher preparation required her to make sure they understood how particular topics could be organized to teach students with diverse interests and abilities. Without a strong knowledge base of curriculum, students, and instructional strategies, Paige knew that Yolanda's instructional decision making and ultimately the learning of each student would be incomplete.

As they began their first meeting, Paige immediately recognized that Yolanda possessed strong content knowledge in mathematics. She wanted to start with Yolanda's questions, so she asked Yolanda, "What are your biggest worries right now about your teaching?"

Yolanda responded, "I can't seem to fit all the pieces into a lesson, and I need help presenting the content so that students pay attention and learn what I intended."

At that point, Paige offered some ideas that had worked for her, but the conversation abruptly ended when the bell rang and Yolanda had to begin teaching her next-period class. Paige left the school, as she had to move on to the next of three schools where her other mentees worked.

As Paige drove out of the parking lot, she thought to herself, "Time is going to be a problem this year. I have mentees in schools across the city and Yolanda really doesn't have too much time to meet with me. I realize she has a young family and doesn't want to stay after school on most days. But I have a feeling she is going to need a lot of help."

Paige's intuition proved true when, shortly after the school year began, Yolanda's principal asked her to work more closely with Yolanda. The principal explained that he had watched Yolanda teaching and that she was having problems with management. He had already sent the department head down to help her become familiar with the school behavior plan, the curriculum standards, and the district's testing expectations. The department head had shared that Yolanda seemed pretty overwhelmed.

Paige thanked the principal for the insight, and the two of them discussed what each of their roles would be related to Yolanda's teaching. The principal noted that he would be responsible for evaluating Yolanda and that Paige would be responsible for supporting her growth as a teacher. If Paige felt Yolanda needed specific help with the subject area requirements, they would meet together with the department head. The principal also noted that he would share concerns with Paige but would not expect Paige to share confidential information with him. He also asked Paige to let him know if there were resources that Yolanda might need for other professional development needs. He was committed to helping Yolanda be successful, and he realized that Paige's responsibilities needed to be kept very separate from his evaluation responsibilities.

This is when Paige began her "interior design" work. Given that the role of an interior designer is often to support and guide clients who have encountered a decorating dilemma, Paige began providing support and guiding Yolanda through her first professional struggle. Paige quickly realized that in order to fully understand the situation, she would have to spend some extended time observing Yolanda's teaching and probe her thinking about planning and delivering instruction. However, she knew that Yolanda's time was at a premium, so she suggested that they communicate by e-mail. Yolanda thought that was a great idea. She could go home to her kids and still get help from Paige. These actions initiated their work together. Just as an interior designer cannot develop a plan without an understanding of the needs of the people who use the space and visualizing the physical characteristics of the space, Paige could not provide appropriate guidance or develop a plan to assist Yolanda without an understanding of Yolanda and her students' needs. As a result, during the two days, they "talked" using e-mail. In those e-mails, Paige probed:

Explain to me the content you are teaching to the kids.

Why is this concept important?

What do the children already know about this concept?

Do they have any prior knowledge related to this concept?

Yolanda's responses to these questions indicated that she knew the content well but less about the children. Paige encouraged her to think about gathering more student learner knowledge and set up an observation time.

After observing Yolanda teaching the math lesson, Paige realized that the dilemma was much greater than she initially imagined. Not only was Yolanda struggling with classroom management, as many novice teachers do, she seemed to have no understanding of how a lesson should flow structurally and was not able to communicate the contents and goals of the lesson effectively to her students. Paige's notes from that day quickly revealed the first design dilemma: "I knew that if I was struggling to understand what she was saying, the students probably didn't understand either. It appeared as if she had done nothing to prepare for the lesson prior to teaching. She was lost and fumbling her way through."

Knowing that Yolanda was expecting Paige to observe that day, it seemed odd that she was not prepared. As a result, in the postobservation discussion, Paige paid particular attention to how Yolanda described her struggles and how she framed her own frustrations within the classroom context. During the postconference, Paige asked Yolanda to get her up to speed on the lesson she observed.

Y: *As I said before, I just can't seem to fit all the pieces into a lesson, and the kids don't pay attention. I don't think they are learning what I intended.*

P: *Over e-mail we discussed the content you were teaching and what the students already know, but we didn't talk about how you used the text to plan. Tell me about that.*

By listening to Yolanda's description about how she used the text to plan and reflecting on her observation, Paige quickly realized that lack of preparation was not the dilemma at all, only the manifestation of a greater issue. Paige thought, "She not only didn't understand how to use the text when teaching a lesson, but she didn't know how to use the math text in planning a lesson. She just assumed you pick it up and go." Based on observation and listening to her "client," Paige immediately identified a focus for her work with Yolanda. The focus must be on teaching Yolanda how to plan instruction. Paige needed to help Yolanda realize that the math text was a resource to accomplish the objective she was required to teach.

Paige knew that she had to act fast in order to help Yolanda survive past the 97 days that would determine her continued employment as a high school math teacher. She had to find a way to provide direct guidance to Yolanda in the area of planning. At present, it was as if Yolanda were trying to host a party in an empty house; there was no furniture, décor, or organization. It was obvious that Yolanda knew the content of mathematics and could apply these math skills for her own personal use, but she did not understand how to translate her content knowledge into pedagogically and developmentally appropriate learning activities for her students, a skill that would be critical for her success as a teacher. As Yolanda's "interior designer," Paige had to help her learn to select appropriate furnishings "from the text," and coordinate interior details "in terms of instruction."

Paige began her work with Yolanda in the planning process by asking Yolanda to describe the challenges she faced. Yolanda shared that the elements of her lessons seemed disjointed and didn't make sense. She said that she would lose her place in the textbook turning back and forth from the "plan" to the activity page and in the process would get sidetracked by something that was happening in the classroom. When the concepts she was teaching relied on students' understandings of concepts taught earlier in the week, the students seemed to not even recognize them.

Paige began with questioning, "Okay, Yolanda, what content needs to be taught this week?" They started charting the concepts out broadly and then they broke the concepts down into subconcepts and talked about how they would then need to link and sequence them. Next, Paige taught Yolanda how to write objectives that targeted the content understandings that needed to be accomplished.

After identifying the objectives, Paige asked Yolanda to describe how she could be sure that each student understood the objective she was teaching. Quickly, Paige realized that there was substantial work to do with Yolanda in the area of assessment. For today, Paige found it easier to point out some assessment tools within the book chapter that could be used to check on student learning each day. She knew that eventually she would like to broaden Yolanda's thinking about assessment but that she wasn't ready for that yet.

Once they had nailed down the objectives and a source of formal assessment for those objectives drawn from the text, Paige offered suggestions by talking aloud about how elements within a lesson flowed in her own lessons when she taught. After providing a couple of possibilities, Paige helped Yolanda understand how to introduce the concepts individually and then integrate several concepts into one activity to maximize her use of time.

As the planning session unfolded, Paige used her assessment of Yolanda's needs to develop a simple planning strategy she could use in future planning. Paige demonstrated how to use the text as a resource to determine objectives, arrange the lesson elements in a coherent order, select appropriate assessment, identify instructional strategies that link to that assessment, determine the materials that would be utilized, and establish a time frame for the instructional elements to occur. In fact, this planning meeting resembled a direct instruction lesson in that Yolanda was guided *explicitly* through the process of planning with Paige as her guide modeling her own thought process at each step.

Thanks to her principal's commitment to providing sacred mentoring time to novice teachers, Paige and Yolanda met before school and during her first-period planning to work on her lesson planning. They identified objectives and assessments as well as photocopied textbook pages and arranged them in a cohesive order. Next, they selected which activities would be most appropriate for each lesson, wrote down the time frame for each activity, and helped each phase of the lesson make sense to Yolanda. Paige did a lot of thinking aloud and modeling of how she might combine some lesson contents to make the best use of time. She also noted the things that she thought about and considered as she planned. As Yolanda watched Paige try to figure out how all the pieces worked together, she began to create a framework in her own mind for making sense of all the pieces. By hearing how Paige thought about planning, Yolanda gleaned how to use the scope and sequence, what to think about in terms of lesson presentation, and how to develop a realistic time frame as a guide.

In previous mentoring experiences, Paige had shied away from explicitly telling her mentees exactly how she would do something, because she did not feel comfortable making her mentees feel as though they had to mimic her personal strategies. Paige still wanted Yolanda to develop her own personal style of planning, teaching, and assessment that was based on her own beliefs, and wanted to allow her the space to do so. However, she knew Yolanda needed something more immediate to help her be successful. Paige felt comfortable offering Yolanda something structured and specific to embrace and use before she began developing and negotiating this planning process on her own. She also told Yolanda that this was a process that would become Yolanda's as she gained more confidence.

As Paige balanced her role of "interior designer," she was careful to make Yolanda "feel at home in the planning space." She didn't want Yolanda to feel as if she would just "remodel and run." Like an interior designer, who consults with clients to design a space conducive to their lifestyle, Paige wanted to ensure that the format for the lesson made sense to Yolanda and fit her own needs as a novice teacher.

As the year progressed, Paige realized that the time she spent with Yolanda was well worth the effort. Yolanda began voicing more of her own ideas and became more confident. Paige continued to use questioning to check in at various points during their sessions and asked Yolanda to contribute her own personal suggestions as they planned together.

Paige would ask Yolanda, "Does that make sense for what you want to accomplish? How could you do it another way? What challenges might you experience in this lesson that should be planned for? How well do your assessments match your objectives?"

Even though Paige had substantial experience working with novices in the past, this experience presented a new challenge that forced her to reconsider her role as a teacher educator. This experience caused her to question the effectiveness of her previous, less direct and explicit, approaches to mentoring. What she had learned as a mentor is that there are times when explicit or direct instruction is absolutely necessary and that if the mentee knows that he or she is working from a caring relationship, things work out fine.

Additionally, Paige learned from this mentoring episode the importance of identifying a problem in a timely manner and providing the time and space to provide appropriate guidance. Paige was able to assist Yolanda "just in time" to be successful for the 97-day review period by dedicating an extensive block of time to help Yolanda develop a deeper understanding of the planning process.

At the district monthly mentor meeting, Paige shared with other mentors about her work with Yolanda. "At first, we spent three hours planning one math lesson. As much as this seemed like an extensive amount of time to spend on one lesson, the payoff was well worth it. In the end, I actually think it saved me time. I think I would rather spend one intensive day with one of my mentees making sure that he or she could plan effectively than have to continuously put out a string of little fires along the way."

Paige also has learned through her own mentoring that there are some things that are just better to tell novices rather than expecting the novices to discover on their own. However, she also realizes that "telling" the novice will not be useful unless the novice recognizes he or she is struggling with a felt difficulty in that particular area. As a result, much of her work as an interior designer now focuses on helping the novice name the felt difficulty.

An important insight is that when one uses the interior designer metaphor, at some level one often does encourage the client (novice teacher) to mimic the designer's own personal style. However, once the basics are there, individual nuances selected by the homeowner make each home unique. Just as the homeowner's décor ultimately reflects his or her different needs and lifestyles, a novice's planning will eventually reflect his or her different teaching needs. Once a mentor provides the essential foundation, the novices can begin to add their own personal mark to the design.

SUMMARY

Mentoring is a complex endeavor. Every mentor and mentee is different. Consequently, every mentor-mentee relationship is different. If a mentor is an interior designer, that mentor will . . .

1. listen carefully for his or her "client's" needs.

2. spend time visiting with (observing) her client (mentee) to understand the mentee's current classroom instructional "space" that is in need of redecorating. In considering the redecorating needs, the mentor must ascertain what the mentee's most

immediate needs are to create a functional and well-designed instructional classroom space.

3. begin with the mentee's most immediate need, providing the essentials to meet that need.

4. recognize that accessorizing the classroom instructional space can come later. In an empty house, essentials (furniture) must come first to make the home functional. Likewise, in an instructional space void of effective pedagogy, lesson planning and organization must come first to get the classroom and teacher functioning.

For Discussion

1. Interior designers use direct and guided instruction to help their clients learn to use their space more effectively while providing specific recommendations for enhancing the utility of the space. Why do some mentors shy aware from directly instructing novices as to how to negotiate acts of teaching (i.e., planning a lesson, how to carry out assessments, or enacting new strategies)? Why is direct instruction the only thing that some mentors do? Is there a balance that can be achieved?

2. It appears that working with Yolanda and the need to provide Yolanda with some direct instruction in lesson planning provided Paige with new understandings about her own mentoring skills. This episode suggests that mentors need to possess a certain pedagogical content knowledge (PCK) of mentoring to carry out their work with novice teachers. Review the definition of PCK presented in Chapter 2. What would be the types of PCK necessary to successfully mentor novice teachers? What does this suggest about the process of learning to mentor novice teachers? How could a mentor enhance their PCK related to mentoring?

3. How might mentors develop a better understanding of the individual needs of their mentees from the outset of their relationship? What are some strategies that mentors might use to engage in differentiated mentoring (adjusting their mentoring to meet the needs of each mentee)?

4. Yolanda's principal was supportive of Paige's work with Yolanda. What would you do as a mentor teacher if your mentee's administrator were not supportive of your work?

(Continued)

(Continued)

5. What components of effective mentoring (creating an educative mentoring context, guiding a mentee's professional knowledge development, and nurturing the development of a mentee's professional dispositions) are evident in this metaphor?

6. List the strength and limitations of conceptualizing mentoring using an interior designer metaphor.

7. Regardless of your own mentoring context, what can you learn from this story to inform your own mentoring practice?

9

Mentor as Real Estate Agent

The Case of Wesley

THE MENTOR

Wesley, a middle-aged African American male teacher with ten years of urban teaching experience at the middle and high school level, mentors out of a deep political commitment and passion for improving city schools. Wesley wants to make schools safe and productive places for all students and teachers. He struggles with his role as a mentor and how his role can contribute to both novice learning and school reform. At this stage of his career, he believes he must help novices understand the needs of the students they teach and create opportunities for novices to feel a part of the school community.

Wesley feels a great challenge is mentoring new teachers who are unwilling or unable to attend to issues of race and class as they teach.

He knows that his role as a mentor must highlight diversity and help others recognize and respond to injustice. His mentoring is highly influenced by his personal commitment to teaching all children:

> As a mentor, I want my teachers to see my passion for teaching all of these children. I was very serious about my teaching, and they need to see teaching as a profession, not a game. Knowing how strongly I feel about it hopefully will rub off on them, and if they don't feel that way, we can work on how to get them to that point. But if they aren't passionate about teaching these children, then I can't make someone love teaching.

Wesley believes that you can't love teaching in this context unless you are passionate about understanding and responding to the needs of urban children.

Recognizing the frustration often elicited by the bureaucracy of urban schools, Wesley knows the value to both students and teachers of a supportive learning community. He believes the urban school bureaucracy can make the work of new teachers feel more like a *game of rules* than a profession that can facilitate important change. Wesley's many years of working in city schools have told him that city schools characterized by supportive learning communities are not necessarily the norm. He also knows from experience that novice teachers will not stay in schools that have unhealthy work cultures and that novices will not be successful if they do not know the "ins" and "outs" of the community where their students learn and live. As a result, Wesley's mentoring focuses on helping novice teachers develop knowledge of the children and community where they live as well as knowledge of how to negotiate and understand the community of their school.

THE MENTEES

Wesley mentors twelve new teachers at his assigned high school. Three of them are male and range between the ages of 23 and 50. The other nine novices are female and range in age between 22 and 44, with the majority of them being career changers under the age of 30. None of the twelve teachers received traditional teacher preparation and, as a result, each is entering through an alternative path to teaching run by the school district and Teach for America. Only three of the new teachers live in the city, and none of them attended a city high school themselves. Only one of the novice teachers is Black, and none of the novice teachers come from families who have struggled economically. Although these teachers do not share the same demographic characteristics as the students they teach, as a part of their application, they each indicated a commitment to urban education and scored either satisfactorily or above in a written assessment designed to predict success teaching in urban schools.

THE CONTEXT

Wesley works within a large urban school district that has had a difficult time recruiting and retaining teachers. As a result, the district created a unique, full-time, school-based mentoring program to support novice teachers. The program provides a full-time mentor to those schools most in need. The mentoring program offers principals a "package deal" by assisting the principal with identifying potential candidates for hiring, providing instructional coaching, and supplying resources to new teachers.

These schools receive intensive, full-time mentoring because they are deemed as highest need. Several characteristics make this full-time mentoring different from other existing programs that attempt to support new teachers. First, full-time mentors are not tied to any one curriculum area such as "reading coach" or "math specialist" and are not responsible for monitoring teachers' use of district-adopted packaged programs. Their only role is to support the development of new teachers. Second, mentors do not report formally to the principal of the school they serve. Additionally, these mentors spend the lion's share of their time working directly with novice teachers in the novices' classrooms.

THE METAPHOR: A REAL ESTATE AGENT

According to Merriam-Webster's online dictionary (n.d.), a real estate agent is "a licensed individual who represents, advises, and negotiates the purchase and sales transaction between the buyer and the seller and receives a commission on the sale of a house." Wesley's work parallels the work of a real estate agent in a variety of ways. He represents, advises, and helps novice teachers negotiate their new positions by introducing them to the community both inside and outside their school building, counsels novices through the process of entering into a new community, helps negotiate "a deal" with the principal to make schoolwide changes that will help his mentees "buy into" teaching in an urban context, and monitors "the deal's" progress.

A GLIMPSE OF WESLEY, HIS MENTEES, AND THE REAL ESTATE AGENT METAPHOR IN ACTION

Wesley began the year with a group of twelve new teachers at his school. The school faced a lot of challenges and so did Wesley and his cadre of new teachers. However, his knowledge of the local educational landscape provided him with insight and focus for his mentoring. The following four scenarios give you glimpses into Wesley's school year and how the real estate metaphor unfolds.

Glimpse 1—Working With the Principal

Wesley had spent the last six months really getting to know Frances Gates #152 High School and its surrounding community. He felt confident that he knew the faculty and staff's strengths and weaknesses as well as some of the assets and trouble spots of the surrounding community. He had really taken his time to get to know people and understand their roles within the school and broader community. Like a real estate agent, he felt comfortable with his knowledge of the "lay of the land" and in his ability to represent his client's needs.

At the end of the first month of his second year at the school, Wesley sat down with the principal, Mrs. Marchman, to discuss his thoughts about the needs of the novice teachers he was mentoring. He had asked all last year for a monthly meeting with the administration and he was pleased that he had finally convinced Mrs. Marchman of the importance of regular conversation between the two of them about the needs of the novice teachers. Wesley's plan was to share themes across the novices that represented their struggles rather than specific details about each mentee, as he wanted to keep his knowledge of specific mentees' struggles confidential.

Given that the culture of the school at this time was far from collaborative, Wesley chose the need for more collaboration as his first theme. He began by saying, "I think the new teachers are feeling good about their choices to be teachers but are struggling to fit in. I heard a lot of them mention that they are often ignored by the other teachers in the hall and that they don't find people sharing ideas and resources. I know they feel lonely."

Mrs. Marchman nodded, as she knew that rang true based on her own observations. Teachers in the school really stayed pretty much in their own rooms and often scooted out right after school. This was a concern of Mrs. Marchman's too. After lengthy discussion about some of the reasons teachers didn't reach out to each other, they realized that they hadn't carved out a realistic block of time for teachers, new and old, to gather and plan together. As a result, they decided to develop some legitimate and important opportunities for teachers to gather together. They began by creating a task force that would begin work to improve the school's collaboration as a learning community.

Another theme that Wesley shared was the novices' struggles with classroom management and his own concern related to safety and discipline. "The school is becoming very unsafe, very chaotic. The halls are not clear this year. I think this is a problem because I hear more and more experienced teachers saying they want to quit."

As Wesley was speaking, he also thought to himself, "I guess that is what I came here to help fix. Now I am finding myself not only mentoring novices but mentoring 'the school.'"

He continued, "At times, I can't concentrate on helping the new teachers learn how to teach because I am spending a lot of time this year on hall patrol, trying to keep kids in order. When I do get in the classroom, I help teachers by taking small groups because the classes are unruly. If I work with a small group while my mentee is working with a group, it allows him or her to get more done and seems to ease *some* behavior issues. However, it doesn't really solve the real problem of discipline and expectations."

Wesley continued his thought, "You see, as long as kids aren't being held to a certain standard by all the teachers in the school, the new teachers are going to struggle. Changing student behavior just because they leave the hallways and enter a classroom is difficult for all of us. I guess I need some suggestions as to how I can help them."

Mrs. Marchman paused for a moment and then began describing a new school behavior plan that was just presented to the principals a few months ago. Although she had liked the plan very much, she hadn't yet initiated conversation and professional development for the staff. Mrs. Marchman and Wesley spent the rest of the hour together talking about how that program could be infused into the school in the next few months.

Although it appears Wesley negotiated every theme that the novices struggled with and that Mrs. Marchman was amenable to all of Wesley's suggestions, this was not the case. If you asked Wesley, he would say, "It is slow going. You just can't go into the principal's office and say 'look, this is what you need to do.' So, I have had to work slowly and get her to trust me and what I am doing. We have built a relationship over time that allows me to share what I see, but she needed to invite me into this relationship. I guess it is like hiring someone to sell your house. She hired me to help her fix up her 'house' so she can sell it to the novices entering the profession. I learned this the hard way. In my last school, I just went in like gang-busters, telling everyone what I thought, and before I knew it, I was at a new school. I guess that principal hadn't hired me to 'sell' his school. My relationship with the principal is the key."

Wesley did leave the office feeling good after his meeting with Mrs. Marchman, as he was prompting some changes in the school community that would ultimately make the quality of the novice teachers' lives better and his job "selling the school" to future novice teachers easier. As a real estate agent would help to negotiate changes for his or her client, Wesley was negotiating the "deal" for the novices in the school.

Glimpse 2—Igniting Conversation About Teaching for Equity

Wesley's real estate work extends beyond the immediate school community as well. Because of his deep commitment to teaching for equity, which he defines as meeting the needs of *all* students, in his Tuesday after school meeting with his group of novices, Wesley probes each of the novice teachers about their current commitment to equity.

After they had each finished sharing, Wesley added, "I really want you to make sure teaching is what you really want to do. Evaluate yourself and see if you are really dedicated to teaching and to teaching these children, because if you are not, then you are going to have a hard time."

He continued, "Some of the teachers in the last group I had admitted that they did not want to teach in this school. The teachers that struggled were those who didn't want to teach in an area where there was a high rate of poverty. They wanted a school that was a little bit cleaner or smaller. They needed to know that if you want to teach in the city, you will most likely be teaching African American children who are poor. They may not live with their parents. Their parents may be on drugs. They may not eat in the morning. They may go to sleep late."

After he had finished, one of the new teachers raised her hand, "I really want to teach these kids but I just don't know what to do when they don't listen. I ask them to sit down and they won't. It is as simple as that."

Wesley responded, "So when you say sit down and they don't sit down, are you willing to find out what is causing them to not sit down? Are you afraid to take the time? Sometimes you have to stray from the system requirements and curriculum to find out what is going on in your class. Because you are not going to teach until these basic needs get sorted out."

He continued, "In my classroom, I used to stop everything and say 'time for a class meeting; what is happening?' The kids can tell you. You can't be *afraid to hear* what is going on in their lives."

Joanna, one of the eleventh-grade history teachers, asked, "I really don't understand what is going on in their lives. Even when they tell me, it is hard to imagine."

Wesley smiled and slapped his leg, "Well, I guess it is time for me to put on my real estate hat and take you on some home visits."

During the next month, Wesley spent his afterschool hours with the novice teachers on community and home visits. He wanted them to understand more about the kids they were teaching and what it would take for them to be successful with these kids.

After the month was over, the group once again gathered for their Tuesday afternoon group meeting. Wesley asked them if they were beginning to know their students better.

Jared responded, "I guess I was shocked to see that on one side of Anthony's home stood an abandoned building and on the other side there were teenage boys who were visibly selling drugs or doing something illegal, and all the other houses were boarded up on the street. I guess now I understand better."

Another novice teacher, Jenna, added, "We went to five houses one day, and I learned something from all of them. This one particular home visit was the one boy that was giving me the most problems. I finally began to understand why the child was causing the problems and understood that he was looking for attention in school."

Although this dialogue by no means resolved all their teaching issues, Wesley had initiated a dialogue around the importance of understanding others who are different from oneself and ignited a conversation around teaching for equity. These conversations remained a thread that extended throughout the year during their Tuesday meetings. Indeed, the novices, led by their real estate agent, began unraveling the demands of classroom management and exploring issues of equity in curriculum. Wesley became a "broker" for the students in the school as he helped represent their lives and instructional needs to the novices he was mentoring.

Glimpse 3—Using Observation to Develop Instructional Knowledge

As the year progressed and the Tuesday conversations about equity continued, the novices asked specific questions about how to be a successful teacher in a challenging city school. Most of them were surviving, but few of the novices claimed they were thriving. How their conversation began follows.

> S: I heard about Mr. Waters, the ninth-grade science teacher. The kids seem to love him. What does he do?
>
> M: Yeah, I also heard about the twelfth-grade writing teacher. She seems to have great relationships with her students.

Wesley listened closely as the conversation began to focus on the novices' interest in exploring some more "real estate." However, this time they were asking to observe other classroom teachers who seemed to be effective teaching in this context.

Wesley left the Tuesday meeting and immediately began the work of organizing observations for the novices and preparing substitute coverage for the classrooms. This was by no means an easy job as substitutes in this school were difficult to come by, but he had some creative ideas to resolve that dilemma, too. He was in the process of setting up a partnership with the local colleges that would provide a pool of substitute teachers for the city schools with full-time mentors. Wesley, himself, also agreed to substitute for his mentees so they could observe other teachers in action.

Each Tuesday meeting that followed began by discussing the novices' observations of these "star" teachers. The conversations included identifying broad themes that cut across these teachers as well as unique qualities and specific strategies that appeared effective in their teaching. After about three months, the interest in observing others declined and the novices began asking Wesley to observe them.

Glimpse 4—Shifting Roles

As a real estate agent, Wesley found himself initially responsible for representing the kids in the novices' classrooms, negotiating the curriculum for these kids, and directly advising the novices as they learned about teaching. He notes, "In the beginning I was their cheerleader, so no matter if they did things wrong or different, I was there to say, 'It's okay, you are learning.' I worked hard to help them successfully 'purchase' this new career."

He continues, "I was much more facilitative in the beginning of the year. I remember when Shannon was trying to get her students to do homework; I was there to offer her suggestions. Other times I would just try to get Shannon to figure out how she can make things better. We worked on lessons or classroom management or communicating with parents or students or other staff members."

During one of the Tuesday classes, Shannon reflected on this shift that occurred during the year between her and Wesley.

She explained, "As the year progressed and I began to take root in my new classroom, Wesley turned the keys over to me. Now he doesn't do the negotiating to the extent he did before. In fact, instead of getting me the resources, he would ask me where I thought I might find that? Or, who I could ask? Or, why do you think he is acting that way?"

Wesley smiled at her description of what had happened during the year. He seemed to nod and looked as if he felt acknowledged. Then he responded, "Well, I am not going to be with you all the time;

you need to become independent, as my goal is to work my way out of my job."

Once the real estate deal had been closed, Wesley was ready to turn over the keys. At that time, his role shifted to that of consultant if the novices had questions from that of central negotiator of their survival and success as teachers in these challenging schools.

SUMMARY

Mentoring is a complex endeavor. Every mentor and mentee is different. Consequently, every mentor-mentee relationship is different. If a mentor is a real estate agent, that mentor will . . .

1. ascertain changes that need to be made in the property (an urban school) to make it more pleasing to the buyers (his mentees).

2. negotiate property (whole school) improvements with the principal to help mentees "buy into" teaching in an urban context.

3. help his mentees get to know and reflect on the community they are "buying into," ensuring that they have a passion for living in, working in, and improving the community.

4. arrange the logistics of visiting potential neighbors (other classroom teachers in the building) to understand how these neighbors have found success and happiness living in the environment.

5. turn "over the keys" to the mentees when they are ready to survive (and thrive) in the urban setting.

For Discussion

1. Wesley spends a good deal of his time as a mentor working with the principal to enact schoolwide changes. Some might view this action as being outside a mentor's domain. Given that the work of a mentor teacher can spread outside of the direct mentor-mentee relationship (especially in a high-need, high-poverty school), how do mentors make decisions about how far they should go to help their mentees? What are the boundaries to a mentor's work?

2. Wesley has an easy time raising issues of equity in education with his mentees and cultivating their commitment to equity, as they see and experience firsthand the gross inequities that exist in education by teaching in this urban high school. How can a mentor who is not mentoring in an urban environment raise discussions that are just as thoughtful and powerful about equity in education with his or her mentees?

3. Taking his mentees on home visits in the community was a critical component of Wesley's mentoring. What do you do if your mentees are reluctant to go on home visits for fear for their safety? How do you help mentees negotiate the importance of understanding a community and their own safety concerns?

4. What does "turning over the keys" mean to you? Do you ever drive the car again? What do you do if you feel your mentee will never be ready for you to turn over the keys?

5. What components of effective mentoring (creating an educative mentoring context, guiding a mentee's professional knowledge development, and nurturing the development of a mentee's professional dispositions) are evident in this metaphor?

6. List the strengths and limitations of conceptualizing mentoring using a real estate agent metaphor.

7. Regardless of your own mentoring context, what can you learn from this story to inform your own mentoring practice?

10

Reflecting on Your Mentoring Practice

The Story of the Artist

I n Chapter 1, we used "The Story of My Mother's Gravy" to introduce the notion that because effective mentoring is complex, there is
no one perfect recipe for mentoring. In Chapter 2, we examined the
components, reviewing what we know constitutes effective mentoring
based on the work of leading researchers and scholars who have studied teaching and learning to teach for years. In Chapters 3 through 9, we
obtained glimpses of seven effective mentor teachers who use different
metaphors to guide their mentoring practice. Coming full circle, we
end this book as we began it, with a story. The story depicts a woman
who wishes to capture the beauty of her grown children before they
leave her home to begin their adult lives.

A middle-aged woman with slightly graying hair entered the café from a side street looking rather pensive. She glanced around the dark room and seemed to squint a bit as her eyes adjusted to the light and she searched intently.

A young man wearing a buttoned shirt and vest asked if she needed any help, and she responded that she was indeed looking for Jean Paul, a local artist, whom she was to meet at that moment. The waiter nodded and turned toward the window, where a wise-looking man sat seemingly entangled in the story before him.

She approached the table and slid the chair under her. "Ah, Marie. I am glad that you found me. I hear you want your daughters to sit for me. Tell me, why is this so important to you?"

Marie replied, "My girls will be leaving me soon to find their own place in the world. They are young women now, each beautiful in her own way. I want you to capture their beauty for me so that I can keep them with me forever."

"So you want me to make them art?"

Marie sighed, smiled peacefully, and replied "Oh, yes."

With that, Jean Paul responded, "I can only do this if I can learn to know each of the girls before I create the art."

Marie agreed.

Months passed, and Jean Paul had spent days with the girls, first getting to know each of them and then creating sketches of their beauty. Finally, the day came for Marie to see Jean Paul's creations. She climbed the narrow stairway that led to the studio over the café where Jean Paul worked.

She knocked and entered. There Jean Paul stood before an incredible painting of the first daughter and a masterful bronze sculpture of the second daughter. Marie gasped, unsure of how to react because she expected to see two paintings hanging before her.

Jean Paul looked questioningly at Marie and asked, "Why do you look so puzzled?"

Marie cried, "I expected to see my two beautiful daughters in paintings and instead I see you have chosen sculpture for one and painting for the other. How will they feel?"

He smiled, "But are they not both beautiful, each in her own right? Do they not capture the essence of each?"

Marie thought for a moment and looked back at Jean Paul's rendering of the two most precious things in her life. Indeed, both of them are beautiful, she thought to herself.

After some time had passed, Marie nodded to Jean Paul, "You have done an exceptional job of capturing their individual beauty. The medium does indeed demonstrate their unique beauty and their own stories."

> *As she stood in front of the pieces reflecting on the lives of the two young women before her, a group of villagers entered the studio. Within moments they were gathered around the mother, expressing great interest in Jean Paul's latest creations. They began studying and comparing the two pieces, drawing similarities and highlighting differences. As they talked, the mother saw in the art the unique beauty of each of her children, how the art demonstrated their different stories and ways of looking at the world to the villagers in the room.*
>
> *The mother knew this was good. She moved to the front of the crowd and shared, "These pieces that Jean Paul created celebrate my two daughters' individual beauty. Instead of making his rendering of my daughters fit the same medium or form, he knew that different media would capture their individual and collective beauty better." Marie believed Jean Paul to be a wise man.*
>
> *Jean Paul watched the crowd from the back of the room.*

This story once again serves as a reminder of the incredible complexity inherent in mentoring. A close and critical look at mentoring is like a close and critical look at art. Quality art takes many different forms, just as quality mentoring can take the form of many different metaphors. By accepting and understanding that different media are most appropriate to represent the unique individuality and beauty of each of her daughters, the woman in the story comes to a better understanding of her daughters, and of art itself. By accepting and understanding that mentoring is as complex an activity as teaching itself, we hope that you have come to a better understanding of your own unique identity as a mentor teacher, and the art of mentoring itself.

BUILDING A MENTOR'S PEDAGOGICAL TOOLBOX

Although visible and present throughout all the metaphors you have explored for effective mentoring, the tools of effective mentoring have not yet been named. As we look across all seven mentors presented in this text, four categories of tools emerge in their work with novice teachers. First, all seven mentors are in constant dialogue with their mentees. A good deal of learning to teach is accomplished through talk. The mentors in this book heighten the productivity of the learning-to-teach talk that occurs with their mentees by employing a number of dialogue strategies. These strategies include the following: probing and questioning; "thinking aloud" to model teacher thinking; asking novices to think aloud; offering suggestions; planning lessons, developing curriculum, and setting goals collaboratively; engaging in active listening; sharing alternative perspectives; paraphrasing a mentee's comments; engaging in electronic discussion; reflecting questions back to mentees for their own consideration; dialogue journaling; and videotaping with the "teacher-cam."

Second, all seven mentors employ observation by their mentees of the teaching act. A good deal of learning to teach is accomplished through watching. The mentors in this book heighten the productivity of the "learning to teach by watching" that occurs with their mentees by employing a number of observation strategies. These include the following: arranging observations of "star" teachers; arranging mentees' observations of their mentors teaching their students; moving mentees through ongoing cycles in and out of the teacher and observer role; using the reflective coaching cycle; coteaching with a mentee and reflecting "in-action;" modeling strategies from coursework; and videotaping lessons.

Third, all seven mentors help their mentees develop understandings of their students and the context within which they teach them. A good deal of learning to teach is accomplished through novices getting to know their students, the school, and the community. The mentors in this book facilitate this process in a number of ways, including the following: arranging home visits and community field trips, using student data to identify mentee goals, enlisting student feedback, using student work to initiate discussion, and engaging mentees in teacher research.

Finally, all seven mentors understand the importance of community and collaboration for novice growth and development, and employ several strategies to build community and foster collaboration. These strategies include the following: developing a protected block of time to meet with novices individually and collectively, creating a lunchtime dialogue group, taking time to celebrate successes, and arranging appropriate mentoring from other key school faculty. Effective mentors realize that learning to teach is so complex that no one mentor teacher could do it all!

Figure 10.1 on the next page depicts a mentor's toolbox based on our analysis of the pedagogical tools that are used by the seven effective mentors in this text. As the most useful toolboxes are well organized, we have sorted these mentors' pedagogical tools into four different compartments. Of course, there is some overlap in the utility and purpose for which a mentor might employ any one of these tools, and each individual mentor will need to build his or her own pedagogical toolbox and decide on the best way he or she might organize the tools of mentoring conceptually.

As you examine the pedagogical tools used by the mentors in this book, think about building your own mentor toolbox. What tools are essential to the type of mentor you have become? How would you organize your toolbox? What tools have you used in your past mentoring practice that are essential to your effectiveness as a mentor teacher? What tools can you borrow from the mentor teachers in this book to make your own personal toolbox more complete? No matter how full your toolbox becomes, the beauty of a mentor's toolbox is it keeps expanding throughout the entirety of your mentoring career. Tools that are missing will be discovered as you continue to reflect on your mentoring practice and read about, think about, and inquire about mentoring.

HOW YOU CONTINUE LEARNING AND GROWING AS A MENTOR

As you finish this book, you may be wondering about the importance of continuing to reflect on your mentoring. No mentor teacher should spend time pondering whether he or she should reflect, because when engaging in the complex act of mentoring, the answer is always an unequivocal and resounding *yes*! There are a number of ways you can continue to learn and grow as a mentor teacher. Three powerful tools we have witnessed for mentor reflection and growth include inquiring into mentoring practice, participating in collegial study groups, and writing about mentoring.

Inquiring Into Your Mentor Practice

Many teachers take charge of their own professional growth and development by engaging in teacher or action research. In fact, many

Figure 10.1 A Mentor's Pedagogical Toolbox

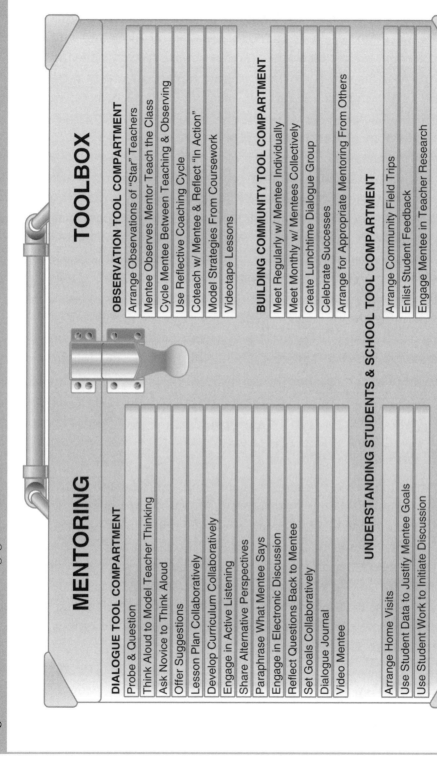

TOOLBOX

MENTORING

DIALOGUE TOOL COMPARTMENT

Probe & Question
Think Aloud to Model Teacher Thinking
Ask Novice to Think Aloud
Offer Suggestions
Lesson Plan Collaboratively
Develop Curriculum Collaboratively
Engage in Active Listening
Share Alternative Perspectives
Paraphrase What Mentee Says
Engage in Electronic Discussion
Reflect Questions Back to Mentee
Set Goals Collaboratively
Dialogue Journal
Video Mentee

OBSERVATION TOOL COMPARTMENT

Arrange Observations of "Star" Teachers
Mentee Observes Mentor Teach the Class
Cycle Mentee Between Teaching & Observing
Use Reflective Coaching Cycle
Coteach w/ Mentee & Reflect "In Action"
Model Strategies From Coursework
Videotape Lessons

BUILDING COMMUNITY TOOL COMPARTMENT

Meet Regularly w/ Mentee Individually
Meet Monthly w/ Mentees Collectively
Create Lunchtime Dialogue Group
Celebrate Successes
Arrange for Appropriate Mentoring From Others

UNDERSTANDING STUDENTS & SCHOOL TOOL COMPARTMENT

Arrange Home Visits
Use Student Data to Justify Mentee Goals
Use Student Work to Initiate Discussion
Arrange Community Field Trips
Enlist Student Feedback
Engage Mentee in Teacher Research

districts across the nation have adopted teacher research as their primary staff development and school improvement mechanism. Teacher researchers define a wondering or burning question to explore about their practice, systematically collect data to give them insights into their wondering, analyze their data, take action for change based on what was learned from their data, and share their results. Just as you may have engaged in the process of teacher research to reflect on your practice as a classroom teacher, this same process can be applied to looking deeply and closely at your mentoring practice.

For example, one mentor we worked with, Don, was passionate about the fact that novices learning to teach in a university teacher education program need to have early field experiences. Because of his passion, he particularly enjoyed mentoring prospective teachers from our university early in their program. Each semester, he hosted a pair of pre-interns, who spent five mornings a week in his classroom. However, as pressure mounted in the state, his district, and his school to have students perform well on the Florida Comprehensive Assessment Test (FCAT), Don began to experience a terrible tension— he was committed to mentoring new teachers, but didn't know how to utilize them effectively during the month of February, where all attention in his school was turned to preparing students for FCAT.

He turned to teacher research to explore his dilemma. He began by crafting an inquiry question: "In what ways can interns be utilized effectively to help my students prepare for a high-stakes test?" In addition to his overarching question, he had a number of subquestions for exploration, including, "In what ways can a focus on preparing students for a high-stakes test be a meaningful learning-to-teach experience for novice teachers?" and "How do I negotiate the tension that exists between my commitment to mentoring and my reluctance to relinquish complete control of every learning experience during the month of February for fear my students, when working with novices, won't get what they need to perform well on the FCAT?"

To gain insights into his wondering, Don decided to use the two mentees in his classroom, Ann and Carla, to do math preassessments with every student. Individual data on every student that indicated where students were strong and weak could be powerful information for designing instruction to prepare students for the FCAT. Logistically, Don could never have collected this data without his mentees' help. Next, Don met with Ann and Carla, and together, they analyzed the preassessments. From this analysis, they ascertained that all the students were very weak in graphing skills, a substantial part of the FCAT. Don and his mentees targeted three areas—how to read a graph, how to make a graph, and strategies for solving word problems using a graph. They decided that given the high-stakes testing environment, they could keep a closer eye on the students' development in these areas if they each worked in small groups. The mentees and Don worked together to design small-group lessons on each component of graphing they needed to teach. Then, for a week, Don organized his morning math time as stations. Simultaneously, a third of the class worked with Don, a third worked with Ann, and a third worked with Carla. Working with a small group, Don, Ann, and Carla could adjust their lessons, being responsive to the children in their groups. As they worked with their small groups, they kept meticulous records on each individual learner and how his or her graphing skills were developing. During the course of the week, all learners rotated through each group.

As Don implemented this plan, he collected data that included the students' preassessments, the lesson plans developed by he and his mentees, records of student learning at each station, and interviews with his mentees that occurred after school at the end of the station week. In addition, Don kept his own journal. When Don analyzed the data, he discovered that novices could indeed be effectively utilized in the month of February and that they could simultaneously learn about teaching by helping to prepare students for a high-stakes test. His mentees learned about planning, using student data to guide instruction, collaborating with others, managing small-group instruction, and classroom organization and management, as well as explored some of the politics and pressures of high-stakes assessment and what that means for teaching. Don stated that had he not engaged in this inquiry, he would never have understood how you can take a bad situation (extreme administrative pressure to focus on FCAT preparation) and turn it into a powerful learning situation for novice teachers. Without engaging in inquiry into his mentoring, Don reflects that he may have just given up his role as a mentor altogether. Engagement in teacher research can be a powerful professional development tool, not only for learning about teaching but also for learning about mentoring.

One of our earlier books, *The Reflective Educator's Guide to Classroom Research: Learning to Teach and Teaching to Learn Through Practitioner Inquiry* (Dana & Yendol-Silva, 2003), may be helpful should you decide to embark on an inquiry into your practice as a mentor teacher. This text may also be suitable for your mentees as you foster their commitment to inquiry, unearthing and examining problems or dilemmas of practice, and ultimately cultivating within your mentee an inquiry stance toward teaching.

Participating in Collegial Study Groups

A second way you might continue to learn or grow as a mentor is through participation in a collegial study group. Collegial study groups serve to connect and network groups of professionals together to do just what their name entails—*study* practice. Critical friends' groups (CFGs) are one example of a collegial study group. The CFGs emerged out of the National School Reform Faculty's work, a professional development initiative that focuses on developing collegial relationships, encouraging reflective practice, and rethinking leadership in restructuring schools. The CFGs provide deliberate time and structures dedicated to promoting adult professional growth focused on student learning. These same structures can be adapted by a group of mentor teachers to focus on mentee learning.

For example, one structure CFGs often use is a consultancy protocol. A consultancy is a structured process for helping an individual or a team think more expansively about a particular, concrete dilemma. The consultancy protocol was developed by Gene Thompson-Grove as part of the Coalition of Essential School's National Reform Learning Faculty program, and further adapted and revised as part of the work of the National School Reform Faculty (Thompson-Grove, 2006). The process takes about fifty minutes and includes the roles of presenter (the person whose dilemma is being discussed by the group) and facilitator (the person who guides the dialogue and makes sure the steps of the protocol are followed).

In the first step of the protocol, the presenter gives a five- to ten-minute overview of the dilemma with which he or she is struggling. Next, the consultancy group spends five minutes asking clarifying questions of the presenter, that is, questions that have brief, factual answers. The group then asks probing questions of the presenter.

These questions are worded so that they help the presenter clarify and expand his or her thinking about the dilemma presented to the consultancy group. During this ten-minute time frame, the presenter may respond to the group's questions, but there is no discussion by the consultancy group of the presenter's responses. At the end of ten minutes, the facilitator asks the presenter to restate his or her question for the group.

The group then talks with one another about the dilemma presented, discussing such questions as, "What did we hear?" "What didn't we hear that we think might be relevant?" and "What assumptions seem to be operating?" During this discussion, members of the group work to define the issues more thoroughly and objectively. The presenter doesn't speak during this discussion, but instead listens and takes notes.

After fifteen minutes, the facilitator calls "time," and asks the presenter to reflect on what he or she heard and what he or she is now thinking, sharing with the group anything that particularly resonated for him or her during any part of the consultancy. Finally, the facilitator leads a brief conversation about the group's observation of the consultancy process.

In our work with mentoring, we met a group of retired educators who were hired part-time by a large district to serve as mentors for six to twelve first-year teachers. This group of twenty mentors met in small groups of four to six mentors once a month. The small groups were formed by the geographic proximity of the schools within which they were assigned mentees. At each monthly meeting, the mentors would share resources, host visits by some of the specialists in the district to become more familiar with the latest district initiatives, and problem solve. When a mentor was experiencing a tough dilemma, they enlisted the help of the consultancy protocol.

One afternoon, Rita confided in her mentor colleagues, "I'm grappling with a very difficult issue that has kept me up at night thinking about it. To organize my thoughts, I've even journaled about it. If we have time this afternoon, I'd like to share it with you all and get some help." The group decided to use the consultancy protocol to help Rita gain some insights into her dilemma.

Rita began, "One of my mentees is really struggling at her school. The majority of the kids in her class read below grade level and really struggle with the required textbook series for reading. She knows that what she is doing is not working, and wants to try to adapt her reading instruction, teaching the same skills that are targeted in the textbook series, but substituting reading material that is more closely aligned with her students' reading level. Yet, she is receiving mixed messages from the principal, the team leader, and the standards coach. The principal tells her she needs to adapt instruction for kids who can't read and she should rely on her reading coach and team leader to help her. The team leader tells her there's no way she can depart from the textbook, as district policy is that every student takes the same theme tests from the textbook series. The standards coach tells her it's okay to depart from the textbook as long as she is still teaching the standards. Enter into this mix Rita, her mentor. I'm struggling with my role in this mess. Is it within my domain as a mentor to advise her? How do I help my mentee figure out what to do?"

The consultancy group received some clarification of the dilemma by asking Rita such questions as, "What school is your mentee teaching in?" "What grade level is she teaching at?" and "Have you met yourself with the reading coach and team leader?" Next, the group moved on to pose some probing questions: "What do you know about this textbook series yourself?" "What do you know about the mentee's beliefs about teaching reading?" "What do you know about her students?" and "What are some of your ideas about how to solve this problem?" Rita answered each question and, at the end of ten minutes, was asked to restate her question for the group. Rita spoke, "How do I help my mentee figure out what to do?" Rita then remained silent as the group discussed the dilemma presented:

> I can definitely relate to Rita's problem. I think sometimes these new teachers are receiving so much advice from so many different people, the advice no longer becomes effective—they're drowning in a sea of support! I think one of our roles as mentors might be to coordinate the support. I think Rita should meet with the principal, reading coach, and team leader together.
>
> I agree with you, but Rita needs to be careful to protect her mentee. It could come across that her mentee is whining because she wants to try something and her team leader won't let her do it. If Rita steps in, it could cause a rift in her mentee's relationship with her team leader.

Another thing Rita might do is meet with the district reading coach and learn more about this textbook series. It might help Rita help her mentee if she became more familiar with the district's adopted reading textbook series. It seems like Rita's really frustrated herself because she doesn't really know what the district curriculum is.

The group discussion continued for fifteen minutes. At times, it was difficult for Rita to remain silent as she listened and took notes. She needed to squash her urge to jump into the conversation! Finally, when the facilitator called time, it was Rita's turn to talk once again. Rita noted that one of the most significant comments that came out in the group's discussion for her was the notion of protecting her mentee's relationship with the team leader. Before the discussion, she hadn't realized the implications her actions as a mentor could have on her mentee's relationship with others in the school. She was only thinking of her mentee's work within the classroom and what she should do with the kids.

Finally, the group debriefed the process. One group member shared, "I found it hard to distinguish between factual questions and probing questions, but I see why it's important to distinguish them from each other." Another member shared, "It was hard for me to follow the protocol and not just jump in and give advice to Rita right after she shared her dilemma." All in all, the group found the protocol to be an extremely valuable tool to help them all reflect on their mentoring.

By its very nature, the work of mentoring is difficult, and can be arduous and painful at times when you find yourself mentoring a struggling novice. By creating or joining a collegial study group focused on mentoring, you surround yourself with other professionals who can provide support and help as you problem solve and get through difficult mentoring times together. Additional information regarding the creation of CFGs and protocols can be found at http://www.harmonyschool.org/nsrf/default.html.

Writing About Mentoring

Reflecting on your practice as a mentor teacher is all about thinking. A wonderful way to *think* about your mentoring is to *write*. Noted educational ethnographer Harry Wolcott (1990) goes so far as to state that "writing and thinking are synonymous: The conventional wisdom is that writing reflects thinking. I am drawn to a different position: Writing *is* thinking" (p. 21).

Furthermore, Mills (2003) states that "the very process of writing requires the writer to clarify meaning—choose words carefully, thoughtfully describe that which is experienced or seen, reflect on experiences, and refine phrasing when putting words on a page" (p. 164). You may learn something very important about your mentee's progress in learning to teach, something you may have missed had you not considered your words on the page, if you write about your mentoring.

Writing about mentoring might simply take the form of a journal, where you note critical incidents or incidentals that occurred as you engaged in the act of mentoring. A mentor's journal can serve as a record of ideas you have related to your mentee's growth and development that might be forgotten if not committed to paper.

Another form your writing might take is a replica of Chapters 3 through 9 in this book. Think about what metaphor you use to conceptualize your practice as a mentor. Present a description of who you are, who your mentee is, and your mentoring metaphor, and provide a glimpse into your interactions with your mentee that exemplify your selected metaphor. This particular piece of writing could remain private, as you discover the strengths and limitations of the metaphors you use to conceptualize practice through this writing exercise, or you may share this piece of writing with others, especially if you are a member of a mentor support group.

A third form writing about mentoring might take is a case study. A case study is a story based on a real mentoring event that caused a felt difficulty for the mentor. The goal of the case is to spur on dialogue when shared with others. A case can be brief or detailed. One example of a case study written by a mentor teacher who was sharing her classroom with a paid apprentice follows.

Patriotism Versus Personal Beliefs

Nancy Samer was mentoring a paid apprentice, Susan, in her eleventh-grade history classroom. Nancy and Susan had become good friends. They had many of the same philosophies and beliefs. They also worked cohesively when coteaching in the classroom. There was a natural flow between the two.

(Continued)

(Continued)

> *During homeroom, Nancy always required students to stand, place their hand on their heart, and recite the pledge. Her class was also required to remain standing and sing the patriotic song after the pledge. Both the pledge and song were broadcast over the closed-circuit system. The only exceptions to this requirement were students who, for religious reasons, were not allowed to pledge. These students were asked to stand but did not need to recite the pledge, place their hand on their heart, or sing the song. In past years, when parents requested that their child not even stand, Nancy abided by this request. Patriotism and civic duty were something very important to Nancy, so she made a special effort to teach both of these to her class.*
>
> *One day during their planning period, Susan opened a conversation with Nancy by stating, "I don't know if you noticed, but I don't say the pledge." Nancy replied that she had noticed and inquired why Susan did not pledge. Susan recounted a story of when she was in high school and had developed a belief that people should not pledge to a thing, the flag. When she did not pledge in school, teachers required her to pledge. Susan's father was eventually involved and the school system was sued. Nancy asked Susan if her belief was based on a religious belief, to which she replied no. Nancy then went on to explain to Susan that patriotism and civic duty were things she felt were very important to teach, especially as an American history teacher. She also explained to Susan that because she was teaching this in her classroom, Susan was not modeling what was to be taught; therefore, Susan was asked if during the pledge she could please stand in the back of the room.*
>
> *Nancy was never really satisfied with the outcome of this dilemma. She has always felt that in a public school, with separation of church and state, students and adults alike should pledge. She had never, in all her years of mentoring new teachers, encountered this situation.*

The act of writing a case study helps the mentor think systematically about a critical event that has occurred. Committed to paper, cases capture some of the more difficult moments in mentoring that can be shared, discussed, and debated with others. Case discussion and debate help everyone who comes in contact with the case learn and grow as educators.

In this chapter, we have explored three ways you can continue to learn and grow professionally in your role of mentor. Whether you use any of these three strategies or other strategies, what is most important is that you do reflect, and through reflection connect to other professionals who can provide support for you as you support the teaching of another. Of course, reflection takes precious time.

Indeed, effective mentoring is a time-consuming and labor-intensive task, and time is something that all educators have very little of!

However, we believe that recognizing and addressing the complexity of mentoring is well worth your time as an educator. Your work as a mentor will have an exponential impact on the children in our schools. In an effort to highlight that impact, we calculated the number of students Kevin, one of the mentors we have worked with and whom you met in Chapter 4, will influence as a result of his mentoring efforts to date.

During the course of this early phase of his teaching career, Kevin has already served as a mentor for eight novice elementary school teachers. For each novice he has mentored so far, he will influence the education of at least 625 children, the number of children the average elementary school teacher would educate during the course of his or her career. Hence, to date, Kevin's work as a mentor will influence the education of 4,400 students. Using this formula, we calculate that mentors who engage in mentoring one teacher each year of their career could potentially influence the instruction of 15,625 children! Your work as a mentor is far-reaching. Through your work as a mentor, you touch the lives of hundreds, and potentially thousands, of children that you will never meet. Given these statistics, no one should underestimate the importance of understanding and enacting their mentoring role. Mentoring serves as a real impetus and stimulus to educational reform. Through your role as mentor, you breathe new life into classrooms, you breathe new life into schools, and you breathe new life into the entire profession of teaching itself. Mentor on!

Chapter 10 Exercises

1. Examine the contents of "A Mentor's Pedagogical Toolbox" as depicted in Figure 10.1. What tools are new to you, and in what ways might you find these new tools useful? What tools seem to be missing? What are the benefits and drawbacks of organizing the tools into the four compartments—dialogue tools, observation tools, understanding students and school tools, and building community tools? What are some other ways a mentor's toolbox might be organized?

(Continued)

(Continued)

2. Think about a dilemma, tension, issue, or problem you are experiencing in your practice as a mentor. Design a research plan to inquire into your dilemma. Include in your plan a statement of your question (or wondering), data collection strategies for gaining insights into your wondering, a plan for analyzing and sharing collected data, and a time line for the completion of this inquiry into mentoring.

3. Practice using the consultancy protocol with a group of mentors to gain insights into a specific mentoring problem. Try using the consultancy protocol with a group of mentees as well, as one novice shares a particular dilemma that is occurring during his or her teaching.

4. Using Chapters 3 through 9 in this book as a guide, write about your own mentoring metaphor. What are the strengths and limitations of conceptualizing your practice using this metaphor?

5. Using "Patriotism Versus Personal Beliefs" as a guide, write a case study that captures one of the felt difficulties you have experienced as a mentor teacher. Share and discuss your case with others.

6. Return to the mentoring platform you created in Chapter 1. Based on what you have read and learned from reading this text, completing the exercises, and engaging in dialogue with others about mentoring, what changes would you now make to your mentoring platform? What might be the benefits of regularly sitting down to return to and reflect on your mentoring platform? How can you ensure that you will continue to learn and grow as a mentor teacher, and garner support as you engage in the difficult but critical work of supporting the learning to teach of another?

References

Achinstein, B., & Barrett, A. (2004). (Re)Framing classroom contexts: How new teachers and mentors view diverse learners and challenges of practice. *Teachers College Record, 106*(4), 716–746.

Assist Beginning Teachers. (n.d.). *What can I offer beginning teachers?* Retrieved May 5, 2006, from http://assist.educ.msu.edu/ASSIST/school/mentor/educmentoring/indexeducment.htm

Ayers, W. (1989). *The good preschool teacher.* New York: Teachers College Press.

Ball, D. L., & McDiarmid, G. W. (1989). *The subject matter preparation of teachers* (Issue Paper 89–4). East Lansing: National Center of Research on Teacher Learning, Michigan State University.

Bambino, D. (2002). Critical friends. *Educational Leadership*, 25–27.

Blase, J., (Ed.). (1991). *The politics of life in schools: Power, conflict, and cooperation.* Thousand Oaks, CA: Corwin Press.

Brownell, E. Y., Yeager, E., Rennells, M. S., & Riley, T. (1997). Teachers working together: What teacher educators and researchers should know. *Teacher Education and Special Education, 29*(4), 340–359.

Cochran-Smith, M. (1991). Learning to teach against the grain. *Harvard Educational Review, 61*, 279–310.

Cochran-Smith, M., & Lytle, S. (1999). Relationship of knowledge and practice: Teacher learning in communities. *Review of Research in Education, 24*, 249–298.

Dana, N. F., & Silva, D. Y. (2002). Building an inquiry oriented PDS: Inquiry as a part of mentor teacher work. In I. N. Guadarrama, J. Nath, and J. Ramsey (Eds.), *Forging alliances in community and thought: Research in professional development schools* (pp. 87–104). Greenwich, CT: Information Age Publishing.

Dana, N. F., & Yendol-Silva, D. (2003). *The reflective educator's guide to classroom research: Learning to teach and teaching to learn through practitioner inquiry.* Thousand Oaks, CA: Corwin Press.

Darling-Hammond, L., & McLaughlin, M. W. (1995). Policies that support professional development in an era of reform. *Phi Delta Kappan, 76*(8), 597–604.

Dewey, J. (1938). *Experience and education.* New York: Collier Books.

Elliott, J. (1991). *Action research for educational change.* Milton Keynes: Open University Press.

Elliott, J. (1997). School-based curriculum development and action research in the United Kingdom. In S. Hollingsworth (Ed.), *International action research: A casebook for educational reform* (pp. 17–28). London: Falmer Press.

Feiman-Nemser, S. (1990). Teacher preparation: Structural and conceptual alternatives. In W. Robert Houston (Ed.), *Handbook of research on teacher education*. New York: Macmillan.

Feiman-Nemser, S. (1996). *Teacher mentoring: A critical review.* Washington, DC: American Educational Research Association. (ERIC Document Reproduction Service No. ED 397 060)

Feiman-Nemser, S. (1998). Teachers as teacher educators. *European Journal of Teacher Education, 21*(1), 63–74.

Feiman-Nemser, S. (2001). From preparation to practice: Designing a continuum to strengthen and sustain teaching. *Teachers College Record, 103*(6), 1013–1055.

Franke, A., & Dahlgren, L. O. (1996). Conceptions of mentoring: An empirical study of conceptions of mentoring during the school-based teacher education. *Teaching and Teacher Education, 12,* 627–641.

Friend, M., & Cook, L. (1990). Collaboration as a predictor for success in school reform. *Journal of Educational and Psychological Consultation, 1*(1), 69–86.

Fullan, M. (1993). *Change forces: Probing the depths of educational reform.* Bristol, PA: Falmer.

Ganser, T. (1998, Winter). Metaphors for mentoring. *The Educational Forum, 2,* 113–119.

Gold, Y. (1996). Beginning teacher support: Attrition, mentoring, and induction. In J. Sikula, T. J. Buttery, & E. Guyton (Eds.), *Handbook of research on teacher education* (2nd ed., pp. 548–594). New York: Macmillan.

Good, T., & Brophy, J. (1994). *Looking in classrooms* (6th ed.). New York: HarperCollins.

Grossman, P. L. (1990). *The making of a teacher: Teacher knowledge and teacher education.* New York: Teachers College Press.

Hicks, C. D., Glasgow, N. A., & McNary, S. J. (2005). *What successful mentors do.* Thousand Oaks, CA: Corwin Press.

Holmes Group. (1995). *Tomorrow's schools of education.* East Lansing, MI: Holmes Group.

Huling-Austin, L. (1990). Teacher induction programs and internships. In W. R. Houston (Ed.), *Handbook of research on teacher education* (pp. 535–548). New York: Macmillan.

Ingersoll, R. (2001). Teacher turnover and teacher shortages: An organizational analysis. *American Educational Research Journal, 38*(3), 499–534.

Kennedy, M. (1991). *An agenda for research on teacher learning* (NCRTL Special Report). East Lansing: National Center for Research on Teacher Learning, Michigan State University.

Kilgore, K., Ross, D., & Zbikowski, J. (1990). Understanding the teaching perspectives of first-year teachers. *Journal of Teacher Education, 41*(1), 28–38.

Ladson-Billings, G. (1999). Just what is critical race theory, and what's it doing in a nice field like education? In L. Parker, D. Dehyl, & S. Villenas (Eds.), *Race is . . . Race isn't* (pp. 7–30). Boulder, CO: Westview Press.

Lakoff, G., & Johnson, M. (1980). *Metaphors we live by.* Chicago: University of Chicago Press.

Levin, J., & Nolan, J. (2000). *Principles of classroom management* (3rd ed.). Boston: Allyn & Bacon.

Lortie, D. C. (1975). *Schoolteacher*. Chicago: University of Chicago Press.

Kenyon, G. M., & Randall, W. L. (1997). *Restorying our lives: Personal growth through autobiographical reflection*. Westport, CT: Praeger.

Mills, G. E. (2003). *Action research: A guide for the teacher researcher*. Saddle River, NJ: Pearson Education.

National Commission on Teaching and America's Future. (1996). *What matters most: Teaching for America's future*. New York: Author.

National Commission on Teaching and America's Future. (1997). *Doing what matters most: Investing in quality teaching*. New York: Author.

National Commission on Teaching and America's Future. (2003). *No dream denied: A pledge to America's children*. New York: Author.

Nolan, J., & Hoover, L. (2005). *Teacher supervision and evaluation: Theory into practice*. Hoboken, NJ: Wiley.

Palmer, P. J. (1998). *The courage to teach: Exploring the inner landscape of a teacher's life*. San Francisco: Jossey-Bass.

Portner, H. (2003). *Mentoring new teachers*. Thousand Oaks, CA: Corwin Press.

Rust, F. O. (1994). The first year of teaching: It's not what they expected. *Teaching and Teacher Education, 10,* 205–217.

Schön, D. A. (1983). *The reflective practitioner: How professionals think in action*. New York: HarperCollins.

Schön, D. A. (1987). *Educating the reflective practitioner*. San Francisco: Jossey-Bass.

Sergiovanni, T. J., & Starratt, R. J. (2002). *Supervision: A redefinition*. Boston: McGraw-Hill.

Shulman, L. S. (1986). Those who understand: Knowledge growth in teaching. *Educational Researcher, 15*(2), 4–14.

Shulman, L. S. (1987). Knowledge and teaching: Foundations of the new reform. *Harvard Educational Review, 57*(1), 1–22.

Silva, D. Y., & Dana, N. F. (2001). Collaborative supervision in the professional development school. *Journal of Curriculum and Supervision, 16*(4), 305–321.

Silva, D. Y., & Tom, A. R. (2001). The moral basis of mentoring. *Teacher Education Quarterly, 28*(2), 23–32.

Starnes, B. A. (2001). Thoughts on teaching: My mother's gravy. *Phi Delta Kappan, 83*(2), 110.

Thompson-Grove, G. (2006). *Consultancy protocol*. Retrieved March 2, 2006, from http://www.smallschoolsproject.org/PDFS/consultant.pdf

U.S. Department of Education. (1999). *Predicting the need for newly hired teachers in the United States to 2008-09* (NCES Publication No. 1999-026). Washington, DC: Author.

Wang, J. (2001). Contexts of mentoring and opportunities for learning to teach: A comparative study of mentoring practice. *Teaching and Teacher Education, 17,* 51–73.

Wang, J., & Odell, S. J. (2002). Mentored learning to teach according to standards-based reform: A critical review. *Review of Educational Research, 72*(3), 481–546.

Wasley, P., Hampel, R., & Clark, R. (1997). The puzzle of whole-school change. *Phi Delta Kappan, 78*(9), 690–697.

Watanabe, T. (2003, Winter). Lesson study: A new model of collaboration. *Academic Exchange Quarterly, 7*(4), 180–184.

Webster's Online Dictionary. (n.d.). Retrieved May 5, 2006, from http://www.websters-online-dictionary.org/

Wolcott, H. F. (1990). *Writing up qualitative research.* Newbury Park, CA: Sage.

Yendol-Hoppey, D. (in press). Mentor teachers' work with prospective teachers in a newly formed professional development school: Two illustrations. *Teachers College Record.*

Yendol-Hoppey, D., & Dana, N. F. (2006). Understanding and theorizing exemplary mentoring through the use of metaphor: The case of Bridgett, a gardener. *ATE 2006 Yearbook.*

Yendol-Silva, D., & Dana, N. F. (2004). Encountering new spaces: Teachers developing voice within a professional development school. *Journal of Teacher Education, 55*(2), 128–140.

Zeichner, K., & Hoeft, K. (1996). Teacher socialization for cultural diversity. In J. S. Kula (Ed.), *Handbook of research on teacher education* (2nd ed., pp. 525–547). New York: Macmillan.

Index

CORWIN PRESS

The Corwin Press logo—a raven striding across an open book—represents the union of courage and learning. Corwin Press is committed to improving education for all learners by publishing books and other professional development resources for those serving the field of PreK–12 education. By providing practical, hands-on materials, Corwin Press continues to carry out the promise of its motto: **"Helping Educators Do Their Work Better."**